COACHING
FOOTBALL

D1056746

Jo

B
BETTERWAY BOOKS
CINCINNATI, OHIO

99   98   97   96   95   5   4   3   2   1

Library of Congress Cataloging-in-Publication Data

McCarthy, John P.
    The parent's guide to coaching football / by John P. McCarthy, Jr. — Rev.
      p.   cm.
    Rev. ed. of: A parent's guide to coaching football. © 1991.
    Includes index.
    ISBN 1-55870-395-0 (pbk. : alk. paper)
    1. Football for children—Coaching. I. McCarthy, John P., Parent's guide to
coaching football. II. Title.
GV959.55.C45M33   1995
796.332'07'7—dc20   95-14391
                                                    CIP

Edited by David Tompkins
Designed by Sandy Conopeotis Kent

To Geraldine Capodiferro
Whose love and caring make everyone feel special.
My mother-in-law, with love.

ABOUT THE AUTHOR

Jack McCarthy, like many Americans, is a sports enthusiast and has played and coached numerous sports all of his life. As a parent, he knows that athletic competition builds self-respect in young people. It also teaches them how to handle adversity and how to succeed. The Parent's Guide to Coaching series was developed by Jack to help parents ensure that their child's experience in sports is a positive one.

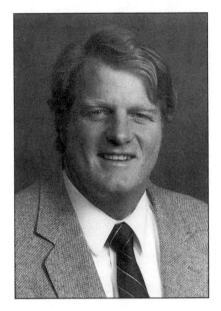

Jack is an attorney and works for the New Jersey Courts. He lives with his wife and three children in Hillsborough, New Jersey. His other books in the series include titles on baseball, soccer and basketball. He also has written *Baseball's All-Time Dream Team.*

INTRODUCTION

"I want to play football, Dad," said my ten-year-old son Joe. He had been thinking about it for a year or so and had now decided to go for it. I knew that he had begun to sense the glory of the game, the popularity, the cheerleaders. I hadn't urged him to play football, as I did with other sports. One reason was that football starts in August, when I usually plan our vacation. I figured he would eventually try out in high school, but admittedly I had some trepidation about his playing before then, particularly while he was in that growth-spurt period from ten to thirteen. Let's face it—it's a rough game. I played and was injured a few times. I have some old friends who are still hobbling around. I guess there is something instinctive in parents that gets us worried about our child playing in such rugged competition.

Anyway, Joe chose to play, and my wife and I chose to support his decision. He signed up for a local Pop Warner team. Most of the other kids had already played for a few years, but Joe made the team and started at fullback. I was happy to see that Pop Warner rules separate the kids so they play against other kids in the same age and weight class. Joe's weight qualified him for the Junior Midgets, 90 to 115 pounds.

I started to think about how I, as a parent, could help my son. It occurred to me, as I watched him at practice and as I considered the game more carefully, that there are dimensions very different from the other major sports. Many skills need to be learned, and parents *can* be very helpful—*if* they are knowledgeable about and can explain fully the various techniques and the basic skills of blocking, tackling, rushing and passing. There are also numerous ways parents can help their child practice these skills. But there are virtually no books geared both to beginners *and* to parents who want to help out as coaches. That's one problem I hope to resolve with this book.

The area in which kids seem to struggle most is in that all-important area of desire and confidence. As I watched, it occurred to me that parents could be most helpful by trying to get their child *properly* motivated to play the game. I get sickened by the way some coaches preach violence to the kids, screaming, "Kill him! Go out there and hurt someone!" I know they are usually just trying to psych a kid up, but I can't see how such guidance is good for young boys. I understand that it's an emotional game, but parents need to ensure that their child gets a correct perspective. That's the second reason I wrote this book.

I have learned throughout my life—in sports, in my professional career, and in my family affairs—that at times things can get pretty rough. But just hanging in there, knowing how to hold on, is sometimes all it takes to make it. I have also learned that tough problems require concentrated effort and reaching down to give it all I've got. And most important, I've learned that I have something extra within me, always there, ready to help out. All sports teach these life lessons, and football, perhaps, teaches them best of all.

Football is not about violence; it's about not quitting. It's about finding that special, extra reserve we all have within us. This is the message of football, and it is the third and main reason for this book. If this book does nothing else, make sure that your child gets that message. Help your son find the good in this game, and also help him to avoid the negatives.

In my three other books on coaching baseball, soccer and basketball, I studiously endeavored to ensure gender-neutral language. These sports are equally for both sexes. I have coached and played sports with both boys and girls. Some of my favorite years of coaching were with a fledgling girls' soccer team that ultimately improved over several years to championship caliber. These girls went on to form the first-ever girls' soccer team at Hillsborough High School in New Jersey. When I think of the favorite athletes I have coached over the years, a mix of boys and girls comes to mind. There is no difference between the sexes in determination, will to win or teamwork.

However, this book *is* written in the masculine. It is merely a recognition of the obvious fact that extremely few girls play football, at any level. If you have a daughter in the game, I apologize. I don't mean to exclude—in fact, I discuss girls in football in my conclusion; however, it seemed senseless to write this book gender neutral since it is so very rare that girls play this sport.

Writing books about youth sports has been a most interesting and rewarding experience for me. The books on baseball, soccer and basketball have all been successful beyond my hopes, and so some kids are surely being helped. That is what it's all about. When writing a book, I find myself more deeply attuned to the inner essence of a sport than when I actually played the sport. Writing this book has given me a new perspective on football, and I hope that by my sharing of it you will be able to help your child, as I have learned to help mine. Go for it!

Chapter One

DESIRE

This is the most important chapter in the book. Don't skip it just because the word *desire* seems obvious or abstract. Desire is the most important aspect of football for both the player and the parent to understand. Without it the child will probably sit on the bench or play poorly. With it he will surely find the game an exciting experience. A player will hear coaches say countless times, "Football is 90 percent desire." Believe it! Desire is the essence of football. If you can find a way to light the fire of desire in your players, you will have helped them in the most meaningful way possible. Watch a game at the younger ages, and you'll see that some of the kids really stand out. They make aggressive tackles or crunching blocks. The better running backs really pop the line, moving low and hard, running with abandon. Other kids are hanging in there, holding their own, giving enough effort to make a decent go of it. Still others seem to be standing around, trying to avoid contact. They are usually not on the field for very long.

The main difference among all three groups is desire. Sure, upper body strength and speed are very helpful. At the high school level the weight restrictions that are in place for grade-schoolers are removed, so sheer size then becomes important. But at all levels the desire to mix it up, to give a good jolt, separates the players from the substitutes. If you can instill or increase this attitude in young men, they will improve their play far more than by weight training, conditioning or learning basic skills.

WHAT IS DESIRE?

Desire is the determination to overcome an opponent, whether by delivering a solid block or by thwarting the block attempt of an opponent and going on to make the tackle. Desire is a state of mind, an abandonment of self, a form of courage, the joy of mixing it up. It is doing one's very best, calling up whatever reserve power is available and never quitting. It is playing both for oneself and for the team's interest. It is the exercise of a determined will, flowing from one's competitive spirit, that drives one to achieve his goal.

The good news is that desire is available to all kids, not just to the gifted few. Sure, some kids already seem to be fully motivated. However, in others desire gets buried under a lack of confidence, or maybe a lack of interest, and so needs to be dug out a bit and fired up. I believe it can be. The unfolding of confidence in a child is truly a joy to behold. Football is quite different from most other sports. As my other books on parent-coaching point out, hitting a baseball, controlling a soccer ball or shooting a basketball requires highly refined skills. Sports such as these require constant practice, repetition and great concentration. While football certainly involves all of these, and I will discuss football skills in great detail later on, football is primarily a game of strength and rugged body contact. The key to football is more in the desire to overcome the individual opponent than in the development of individual skills.

DEVELOPING THE RIGHT ATTITUDE

The good news is that parents and coaches can help bring forth this attitude by communicating and talking over certain concepts with their child.

If a player is already highly motivated, then there may be little need to increase his desire. He has already won more than half the battle, and the joy of the game will be his. However, particularly at the very young ages, most youngsters are at least a bit hesitant about the game, and so they can benefit greatly from some communication. Talk it over! Here are some approaches to consider.

Legalized Roughhouse

Football is legalized roughhouse! It's quite helpful and positive for kids to look at it that way. It's a chance to go out on the field for a couple of hours and romp and tumble. It's really not about violence or anger, as some coaches unfortunately teach the kids. It's not about "going out there and hurting somebody" as some coaches

FIGURE 1
REQUIRED EQUIPMENT

The protection is quite thorough. Neck collars, elbow and forearm pads, and shin guards are not mandatory, but should be worn. (Courtesy NFSHSA.)

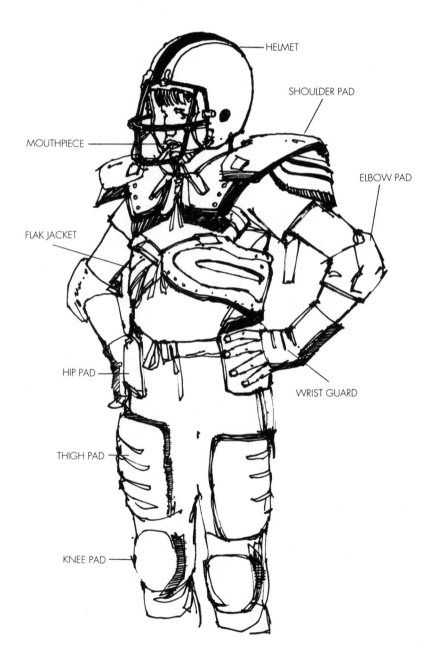

HELMET

SHOULDER PAD

MOUTHPIECE

ELBOW PAD

FLAK JACKET

HIP PAD

WRIST GUARD

THIGH PAD

KNEE PAD

yell (although, in their defense, most times they don't really mean that; they are just trying to fire a boy up). It's just good, clean rough-house. Help a player understand the difference, particularly if his nature is not very aggressive. You don't want to change his nature, and you certainly don't want to make him violent. You just want to teach him that it is possible to reach down within himself and bring forth an exuberance, a sense of personal strength, an indomitable pride, and an intensity of spirit.

Some kids shrink from all of the violent talk, so discuss the matter in a straightforward way if he is hesitant or struggling. Tell him that football is just about romping, about pride, about teamwork. It's a fun free-for-all. Yes, he needs to hit hard. Yes, he must concentrate and be explosive, but it's not about meanness. Channel his perception and energy in a positive way, and he will respond as if a weight has been lifted from him. He will begin to look forward to the next game with a fresh, new purpose.

Full Protection

Football equipment today is quite good. Helmets have a special, scientifically developed lining that completely protects the head. The knees, hips, ribs, thighs, shoulders, and often even the elbows are safely padded. (See Figure 1.) Weakness at the ankle, wrist, shin or neck can be further protected with tape, wraps or a collar. Neck collars are not mandatory, but I recommend parents buy one if one is not issued with the gear. The point is that the kids are very well protected. A player needs to understand how well protected he is, since that understanding will lessen any reluctance to really drive or slam into an opponent. Kids are not very heavy in youth leagues, especially in the first several years, and they don't have enough strength or size to give a really crunching lick, so injury is much less likely than in later years.

I've coached and played a lot of sports, and frankly, I've not seen many more injuries in football than, for instance, in soccer or basketball. I believe there are two reasons for this: One is the protective gear, and the other is the more rugged conditioning that regularly occurs in football. Talk about this. Of course, there are no guarantees—football *is* a contact sport.

Most children have a basic fear of getting hurt that limits their aggressiveness. Fear is usually the greatest obstacle for any young athlete in almost all sports. But the protection players have is excellent, and they can and should rely upon it. Point out how well protected he is and that injuries are rare. Tell him there is no need to hold back.

Never Quit!

Football comes down to one-on-one competition. On any given play, most players on the field are locked in combat with a single opponent. Sure, double-teaming and other maneuvers can require contact with several opponents, but most play is one-on-one, and often it's against the same opponent for most of the game. Sometimes the opponent is stronger, sometimes not; it varies. Usually the coaches spot a mismatch and stay away from it or double-team a strong player. Regardless, your player has a decision to make.

There will be times when he is playing against a stronger opponent. But no matter how strong the opponent is, if he does his best, he will at least slow his opponent down. It's okay not to be able to succeed in every play. It's just never okay to give up. Another teammate may be able to open a bigger hole on the other side, as long as he can hang in there. Even if he is getting beat, he can't quit. He has to give it his best, try to find a weakness, mix up his approaches, try different things. A good opponent usually plays well, but there is great pride in knowing that you did your best and, by hanging tough, prevented the good player from completely having his way. It's also consoling for youngsters to know that they are not expected to do what they can't; they are only expected to do their best and to not quit. More often than not, with increased desire alone, they can find a way to overcome the obstacle.

Play Until the Whistle

Often a kid stops when the play goes to the opposite side of the field. Nothing looks worse to the coach than a player standing still and watching the action (particularly if the game has been filmed).

He must continue until the whistle blows. He should run toward the play and stay animated—do anything except stand and watch. This attitude helps keep his desire up. It also helps keep him free of the coach's anger. Sometimes, the play will reverse back toward him, and in that case continued effort can be quite important to the team.

CONFIDENCE

Confidence is a most elusive quality. Football is a sport that builds it. The coaches yell and bark a lot, kind of like the military, but the idea is to get the kids to wake up. Most kids will get yelled at and be upset by it. Parents will be worried by it and begin to feel protective. The coach is just trying to motivate the player, to toughen him up, to prepare him, and to get him excited enough to put a hard hit on someone. Players often are surprised by what they can really do when they get riled up by the coach. Sure, some coaches overdo it, and there are certainly problems if a hostile coach arouses the wrong feelings, but usually it's for the better. Once a kid sees what he can do, he'll keep on doing it. The coach is trying to get him to the point of giving himself a chance.

The antagonist of confidence is fear. Let's face it, we have all experienced it. Some people live with it daily. It's a part of life. The ability in life to overcome or transcend fear is one of the keys to survival and ultimately a key to happiness. Each player has his own fears, and football will help bring him to terms with some of them.

A kid naturally worries about trying something new—will he be good enough, will he be able to take it? He finds himself flat on his back a few times; the coach yells; he is embarrassed. He gets back up. He keeps going. In a few weeks, he makes a big play and he starts to realize that much of the problem was just his own fear and self-doubt. He learns that he can overcome these insecurities with determination, hard work and perseverance. He has found life's greatest friend . . . confidence. I've seen football lead to this, and it's a good thing.

Chapter Two

WHAT IS FOOTBALL ALL ABOUT?

Football is an intensely physical game in which two teams try to forcibly advance a ball against each other. It is played on a field that is 100 yards long and about 53 yards (160 feet) wide. The field is marked off in increments of 10 yards from the goal line (or zero yard line) on one end, up to the 50 yard line across the center of the field, and down again to a goal line at the other end. There is a 10-yard end zone at each end of the field. (See Figure 2.)

The main idea is for one team, called the offense, to carry the ball into the other team's end zone, scoring a touchdown worth six points. The other team, called the defense, tries to stop the offense by tackling the ballcarrier and bringing him to the ground. Note that each team advances toward *the other team's* goal and defends *their own* goal.

THE CONCEPT OF DOWNS

One of the toughest things for people to understand about football is the concept of downs. Once a team gets possession of the ball, they must advance it at least 10 yards in four attempts, beginning where they got the ball. If they succeed, then they get four more attempts to go another 10 yards from the point of the last tackle.

Each attempt, or play, is called a *down*. Therefore, *first down and ten* means that the next play is the first of the four attempts and all 10 yards need to be made. Similarly, *third down and two* means that the next play is the third attempt in the series of four downs and 2 yards are still needed to make the 10 yards. If the offense gains 5 yards on the next play, then the team has succeeded and maintains possession. They are awarded another first down. Therefore, they get four more attempts to advance another 10 yards,

FIGURE 2

DIMENSIONS OF A FOOTBALL FIELD

(Courtesy of NFSHSA.)

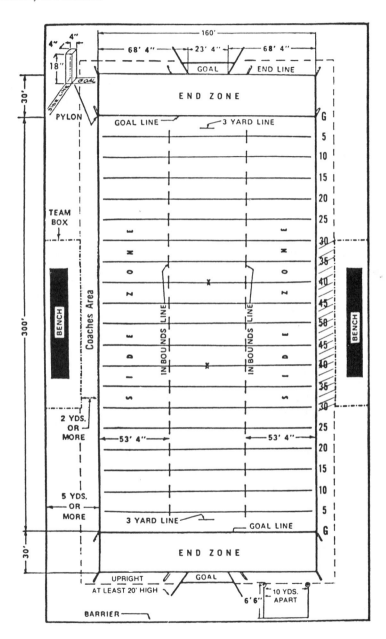

and so the next play is called first and ten again.

This can be difficult for the beginner. Let's try once more! Suppose my son's team receives possession on a kickoff and they begin on their 20 yard line. They need to go 80 yards for a touchdown. However, the rules of football require that the team worry about 10 yards at a time. His team has four chances to get the ball the 10 yards, to the 30 yard line; so it's now *first down and ten*. If they advance to the 30 yard line in four plays they keep possession of the ball and get four more chances to go another 10 yards.

Okay, let's take it step-by-step starting back at the 20 yard line. Let's say our fullback carries the ball forward for 3 yards. Then the next play is referred to as *second down and seven* because it is the second try and they still need 7 yards to get to the 30 yard line. Then let's say that a pass play gains 5 more yards. So, now it's *third down and two* since the ball is on the 28 yard line after two attempts. Then my son catches a nine-yard pass. (Why not? It's my book!) Now the ball is on the 37 yard line. Since the team passed the 30 yard line as originally required, they now have another first down and 10 yards to go. The ball is on the 37 yard line and they have four tries to get it to the 47 yard line.

Now suppose my son had dropped the ball rather than catching that nine-yard pass. Then, it would be *fourth down and two* back on the 28 yard line. The team has one more chance, and if they fail, the other team gets the ball right there. Usually, when a team is so near their own goal line they decide to punt (kick) the ball to the other team so the opponents will have farther to go for a score. That is why most teams punt on the fourth down. Note that a team does not need to use all four plays to advance 10 yards. For instance, if it's first down and the team passes for 20 yards, then it's first down again at the new spot.

MOVING THE BALL

Each team has eleven players on the field. The team with possession of the ball is called the offense and must have at least seven players spread along the line of scrimmage where the ball is. The *line of scrimmage* is an imaginary line that runs from the ball to each sideline. This leaves the quarterback and three other players who are running backs or wide receivers. The player in the center of the line hikes the ball back to the quarterback. The ball may then be advanced by running it forward or by passing it to a player. A play is over when a ballcarrier's knee touches the ground (in youth ball), when a pass is not caught, or when the ball is run out-of-bounds.

After the ball is hiked to the quarterback, he usually hands it off to a running back whose job is to advance the ball forward on the ground toward the goal line. The quarterback instead could pass it to a receiver who catches it and then tries to advance it farther. The quarterback may pass forward or sideways but he must be behind the scrimmage line when passing forward.

The idea for the defense is to tackle the ballcarrier or to prevent a pass by batting the ball away. The blockers try to interfere with the tacklers. They may push with the hands but cannot grab or hold the defense. The defense is free to move as they please just prior to the hike and may play quite fiercely. They may shift around to confuse the blockers. They may freely shove or throw blockers to one side with the hands. The use of the hands by the defense against a blocker is virtually unlimited.

A *touchdown*, worth six points, occurs when the team carries the ball across the goal line of the opposing team or catches a pass within the end zone. Scoring a touchdown also allows the team to attempt a point after touchdown—either by kicking the ball through the uprights of the goalpost, worth one point, or by carrying the ball across the goal line from a certain distance, worth two points. The Pros adopted the two-point conversion in 1994. In youth ball, this scoring is often reversed. Since kicked points are more difficult for young kids, two points are awarded, and running the ball across the goal line is worth one point.

Another way to score besides crossing the goal line is to place-kick the ball between the goalposts and above the crossbar of the goal on the end line. This is called a field goal and scores three points. It usually occurs when the team with the ball faces a fourth down and the ball is within 30 yards of the end zone. If the coach feels that the odds are against getting another first down, he may try for a field goal. This rarely happens at the pre-high-school level of play.

Each team tries to score, and after a total of forty minutes of play (forty-eight in high school and sixty in the Pros), the team with the most points wins.

MAJOR RULES AND INFRACTIONS

As a general rule, however, actions that are intended to hurt or maim, such as spearing with the helmet, punching the head with a fist or forearm, grabbing a face mask, kicking or tripping, or jumping onto a pile of players, are considered to be serious infractions. These actions generally can lead to fifteen-yard unsportsmanlike conduct penalties or even an ejection from the game.

There are many more rules in football. I will review the main ones below. If you want all of the details then you should obtain a copy of the rules from the National Federation of State High School Associations, 11724 NW Plaza Circle, P.O. Box 20626, Kansas City, MO 64195. For college rules write to the NCAA at 6201 College Boulevard, Overland Park, KS 66211.

My objective here is to discuss the major rules so that they make sense to you, particularly if you are a parent and not a coach. In doing so, I may omit certain nuances in an effort to promote your general understanding. In this regard, my review may be technically insufficient from time to time. I advise you to get a copy of the actual rules for technical precision. The actual rules are worded quite technically, as they have to be to cover all sorts of situations. Coaches will need to read them carefully. Much more detail regarding some rules is in the Appendix at the end of this book.

Offside

This infraction occurs frequently and covers several violations associated with players' actions at the moment of the hike. One example is called a *false start*. The basic rule is that offensive personnel must be in a ready or set position (i.e., hands on or near the ground) for a full second before the snap of the ball. Once in the set position an interior lineman may not move his hands or make any other

FIGURE 3
OFFSIDE

Note the ball still on the ground and two players have crossed the neutral zone.
The defensive player could get back, but the end is offside.

sudden movement. The purpose for this rule is to protect the defense from being "pulled" across the line of scrimmage by the movement of a lineman, since offensive motion ordinarily signals that the play has begun. If an offensive lineman jerks, a defender will charge forward. Defenders are taught to move as soon as a lineman moves. So the offensive lineman cannot move until the ball is snapped. Another purpose of this rule is to make sure that the offensive player does not get any more of an edge than he already has since he knows when the ball will be hiked. He cannot cross the line until the ball is hiked. What usually happens in youth football is that a kid forgets the cadence number for the hike and leaves on "one," when the ball is not hiked until "two." (See Figure 3.)

The center, or snapper, may move the ball to get a grip on it, but may not pick it up, stand it up, or jerk his head or shoulder. The running backs must also be set for a full second before the ball is snapped, although one of them may be in motion sideways or backward as the ball is snapped. An offensive player who is not set for the full second before the snap is said to be in *illegal motion*. These infractions receive a five-yard penalty.

Encroachment

This infraction is another form of offside and is generally the defensive version of it. However, it pertains to all players. Picture an imaginary band the length of the football crossing the field between the two teams. This is called the *neutral zone*. No player except the center can have any part of his body in, on or over this neutral zone when the ball is snapped. If a defender crosses this zone and gets back on his side without body contact before the ball is snapped, he is okay.

Remember, only the offensive interior linemen (the center, guard and tackle) are frozen before the snap. The defense can be moving as much as they want, so long as they are not encroaching when the ball is snapped. As noted, the center—the snapper—may have his head or hand in the neutral zone, but not beyond it. Again, the basic idea here is to have everyone separated by at least the length of the ball before each play. Encroachment carries a five-yard penalty.

Holding

Teams are often called for holding during a game. Holding is called against any player, but most often against an offensive lineman who uses his hands or arms to hook, lock, clamp, grasp, encircle or hold in an effort to restrain an opponent (other than the runner). Holding carries a ten-yard penalty and has taken the momentum out of many an offensive drive.

Illegal Blocking

You cannot block an opponent below the waist or *clip* him, to block below the waist *and* from behind, except in what is called a free blocking zone (4 yards laterally and 3 yards deep from the ball). (See Figure 4.)

Legal blocking occurs when clenched hands are in advance of the elbows but not extended more than 45 degrees from the body.

FIGURE 4
FREE BLOCKING ZONE

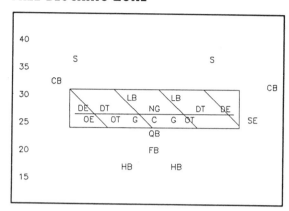

The free blocking zone is an area 8 yards wide by 6 yards deep, centered on the ball.

If extended, the hands must be open and in front of the blocker's and opponent's frames. If the blocker makes initial legal contact above the waist and in front of the opponent and then either slides down below the waist or the opponent turns and continuous contact is made with his back, the block is legal.

Pop Warner Football

Chances are most kids will play Pop Warner football although there are other youth football organizations as well. Pop Warner rules sort out kids nicely according to weight and age groups with an eye to ensuring equality. Figure 5 is a schematic that sets forth the various groupings. Most leagues play the Pee Wee, Junior Midget and Midget groupings. "Older/lighter" means, for example, that a fourteen-year-old who weighs under 115 pounds can play Midget level ball, even though this is usually for eleven to thirteen year olds. Every player must play at least four scrimmage plays per game. A kicked point after a touchdown is worth two points while a pass or run into the end zone after a touchdown is only worth one point. Games are played for four ten-minute periods. The rules are strongly formulated to avoid running up big score differentials between the teams. Other than that, the rules are similar to high school rules.

FIGURE 5

POP WARNER AGE/WEIGHT SCHEMATIC

1988–89–90 POP WARNER TACKLE FOOTBALL AGE/WEIGHT SCHEMATIC

Division Name	Basic Ages	Additional Ages Player Born On Or After August 1st Current Year	Allowed When Older/Lighter Player	Certification Weight Range	End of Season Maximum
MITEY-MITE	7– 8– 9	10		40– 75 lbs.	81 lbs.**
(older/lighter)			10*	40– 55 lbs.	61 lbs.**
JUNIOR PEEWEE	8– 9–10	11		50– 85 lbs.	91 lbs.**
(older/lighter)			11*	50– 65 lbs.	71 lbs.**
PEEWEE	9–10–11	12		65–100 lbs.	106 lbs.**
(older/lighter)			12*	65– 80 lbs.	86 lbs.**
JUNIOR MIDGET	10–11–12	13		80–115 lbs.	121 lbs.**
(older/lighter)			13*	80– 95 lbs.	101 lbs.**
MIDGET	11–12–13	14		90–135 lbs.	141 lbs.**
(older/lighter)			14*	90–115 lbs.	121 lbs.**
SENIOR MIDGET	12–13–14	15		95–135 lbs.	141 lbs.**
(older/lighter)			15*	95–115 lbs.	121 lbs.**
JUNIOR BANTAM	12–13–14	15		110–150 lbs.	156 lbs.**
(older/lighter)			15*	110–130 lbs.	136 lbs.**
BANTAM	13–14–15	16		125–165 lbs.	171 lbs.**
(older/lighter)			16*	125–145 lbs.	151 lbs.**

*The asterisked (*) provisions in each division allow the so-called "overage, but underweight" player to also qualify, if born on or after August 1st of the prior year and not later than July 31st of the current year, thereby allowing the League Age to encompass four (4) years. However, the fourth year of eligibility (older/lighter player) falls under more stringent weight restrictions, per above.

**For all games played after Thanksgiving weekend, either Method A or Method B (see pages 23–24, Article 15, "In-Season Weight Increase") may be utilized, up to a maximum of seven (7) pounds.

Chapter Three

BASIC SKILLS

Certain basic skills must be learned and then executed on every single play. Blocking and tackling are probably the most important, since on nearly any given play twenty-one of the twenty-two players on the field are doing either one or the other. Each player must learn how to block or how to tackle, and if he learns both, he may play on both offense and defense. Passing, running, receiving and pass defense are also major and essential football skills. Then there are specialty skills such as punting, placekicking, snapping the ball, and handling other special teams positions.

As mentioned in chapter one, the desire to overcome the opponent is of primary importance. However, poor skills can greatly reduce the effectiveness of individual effort. An informed coach or parent can be most helpful in this respect, particularly with regard to proper form. Help each boy with the details of technique *before* he develops bad habits that will take years to change.

Often, with thirty or more players on the field at practice, the coach may not notice flaws in each player's form, or he may not communicate clearly to each child the technique and the concept behind the correct form. Here is where a parent can help. Focus on form at practice or at a game. Scrutinize his stance, the height of his attack, whether his legs are digging forward, where his hands and forearms are positioned, how long his effort is sustained, and other areas covered in this chapter. I have also included some drills you can use to work on form.

Frankly, I think videotapes of practices, scrimmages or games are very effective tools for teaching. I don't think they are used much below high school level to teach the players. Yet, I believe videotaping players is an excellent method for reviewing form and execution. I've used it and it works well. Zoom in as close as possible. Then, when you view the tape later, look at my checklist of techniques and review and discuss each one. There may be no better coach than a player's own eyes and his ability to see his errors with your help and correct them himself.

BLOCKING

Blocking is the attempt to prevent a defenseman from tackling the ballcarrier, preferably by removing him from the play, but at the very least by interfering with his ability to tackle. Blocking is done by everyone on the offense, but it is the primary job of offensive linemen, especially the five interior linemen. They are the unsung heroes of the game. Even a defensive lineman will hear his name on the loudspeaker when he makes a tackle, but it's rare that an interior offensive lineman gets public credit for the great block that led to a touchdown. These players must learn to play just for the personal satisfaction of being part of a team and of overcoming their opponent. Sure, there is less glory, but the true fan of football knows that all positions on the field are of equal importance. Running backs know that they live or die based on the performance of their linemen. Linemen do a tough job, and they have to love it. I know—I was one of them when I played.

One day early in the season a player will go home disappointed when he finds out that he has been assigned to a line position. Chances are it's because of insufficient speed. He'll get over it. Don't make a big deal out of it. He is part of a team and should focus on being as good as he can be wherever he is needed.

Often, at the youngest ages the most yardage is gained by a speedster just running wide around the whole pack, since the blocking up the middle is often ineffective. The kids are just learning blocking techniques. If you look at the interior linemen, you will see the kids standing straight up, seemingly just leaning on or pushing each other. With such poor blocking form, a hole for the running back is not formed. As the boys mature, their blocking is much improved, and dive plays up the middle become more effective. In later chapters, I will discuss blocking as it relates to each position and as it relates to overall offensive strategy. However, the basic techniques for blocking are set forth below.

The Blocking Stance

The whole idea of the correct stance is to give the blocker a good start. Each part of the stance is designed to increase a player's potential to overcome his opponent. He must be able to get low enough so he can make it under the opponent's center of force, which is under his shoulders, and yet still have enough power and balance to jolt the opponent, raise him and sustain the block. It's a tall order, and good form helps.

Ready and set positions. A lineman descends into his "set" position, or blocking stance, from an interim stance, called the *down* or *ready* position. (See Figure 6.) After breaking from the huddle where the play is called, he sets his legs a few feet back from the line of scrimmage. The legs are spread about as wide as the outside of the shoulders, with one foot back a few inches. Hands are on the knees, and the eyes are straight ahead. Upon command of the quarterback, the lineman snaps down sharply into the *set* stance, from which he commences the block. The object of the ready position is to ensure that the snap movement into the set stance is smooth and deliberate. Once a lineman is in the set posi-

FIGURE 6
READY POSITION
The ready position, about to descend into the set position.

tion, he may not move again until the ball is snapped. Therefore, the movement into the set position must be exact. It is a twofold motion; the back foot drops back a few inches and the hand on that side drops to the ground into a three-point stance. Once his knuckles touch the dirt, a player cannot lift them again without incurring a penalty.

Feet wide apart and balanced. In the set stance, a lineman's feet should be spread at least shoulder-width apart. (See Figure 7). If his feet are too close together, his opponent will more easily be able to shove him to one side. Action in the middle of the line is heavy and a player can easily be hit from the side and knocked off-balance. The toes may be pointed slightly outward for power and balance. However, with legs spread, the blocker has greater lateral balance. The weight mainly rests on the front or balls of the feet. The toes of the back foot are even with the heel of the front foot, although this can vary according to the player. Taller players often set the back foot farther back than do shorter players. The back foot should not be adjusted once in the set position, since any

FIGURE 7
CORRECT STANCE SET POSITION:

Tail not too high, back straight, head up, weight moderately forward, legs bent. Eyes forward, down hand inside back leg, legs spread nicely, coiled.

movement can be viewed as intention to draw the defense offside.

The back foot is the power foot, and it drives into the strength and thrust of the opponent. It is also the first foot brought forward for balance and to sustain the block. Theoretically, the back foot should be the right foot for those on the right side of the line and vice versa on the left side, but it is also important to be comfortable and feel balanced. Kids usually drop the right foot back no matter what side of the line they're on. A good drill is to have him squat with his feet in the set position and roll around his body weight on them. He can find the foot position that seems to give the best balance for his body frame. This drill also strengthens the lower legs.

Three-point stance, weight moderately forward. The hand on the same side as the back foot snaps down to a point on the line just inside of the back foot and just forward of the shoulder. The weight is rolled forward; the knuckles are down and the thumb is back. Some kids like to balance on their fingertips, but the knuckles give much more stability. The weight should be moderately forward on the hand, just enough so that the player would fall forward slowly if this hand were suddenly removed. With sufficient body weight forward, the player can get a fast start and build momentum quickly. However, with too much weight forward, the player cannot react sharply to defensive movement, particularly stunts, and he cannot pull laterally if that is his assignment. The other forearm should rest comfortably on the thigh. However, it is not forgotten. It must be poised, fist clenched, ready to drive forward and up into the opponent's chest. The three-point stance is recommended, especially for offensive linemen. It's very tough to pull, trap, cross block, or adjust to stunts from a four-point stance.

Back straight, tail down. The idea behind the stance is to create a low, coiled position from which to launch the shoulder forward, under the opponent's shoulder, and to generate enough power to lift and thrust the opponent out of the way. If the back legs are not bent enough, then they are not coiled with maximum power. (See Figure 8). Furthermore, straight legs lift the tail up higher than the shoulders and this detracts from the forward thrust,

FIGURE 8

INCORRECT STANCE SET POSITION:

Head too far down, tail too high, legs too straight and too close, weight too forward.

wasting energy in a downward motion. Finally, it is hard to keep the head up if the tail is too high, and a lowered head limits vision. The tail should be even with the back, or even slightly lower, for maximum effect. However, if the legs bend or squat too far then the player loses time and effort to straighten them out.

Another common problem with the young player is that his back is rounded. This also happens when the legs are not bent enough or spread far enough apart. If the down hand is not far enough out in front of the shoulder it can also result in a rounded back. In effect, the player is merely bending down from the waist. This is a very weak position, and it is dangerous since the head is also down too low. Make sure that the back is straight and parallel to the ground.

Bull the neck, eyes forward. Looking straight ahead is critical. The defense, especially the linebackers, are trained to look at the eyes of the offense for clues to where the play will go. Your player certainly does not want his opponent to know that he intends to block him. The element of surprise gives an important edge to the offense, so an offensive player must learn not to tip off the defense by looking at the person he will block, or by looking to the side the ball will go to. It is especially important not to lean in the intended direction of the play. A blocker should angle his thrust to the left or right depending on the path of the ballcarrier, but he must not do this before the ball is snapped. A "poker face" is important, so discuss this. Tell him to bull his neck, bracing it for contact; keep his head up and chin forward; and give away no clues!

If a player does not bull the neck and instead allows it to tilt or look downward, two things can happen. First, he doesn't fully see the defender and can lose him or have him slide off more easily. Second, he could strain his neck upon contact. A blocker needs to develop the habit of bulling the neck on every play.

The Blocking Charge

Explode with the snap. The most important moment in blocking is the first split second after the ball is snapped. The offense knows exactly when the ball is to be snapped by the center to the quarterback, but the defense does not know this. The quarterback calls out a cadence of signals and ends with a series of hikes, such as "hike, hike, hike" or "hut-one, hut-two, hut-three." He has already told the players in the huddle which of these numbers will signal the snap.

This is a valuable opportunity. It is the "edge" the offense has—the element of surprise. The blocker can set his angle and charge forward before the opponent moves. He can, particularly if the target is directly in front of him, strike with full momentum before the opponent has a chance to build up any momentum. Therefore, a quick charge at the same instant as the snap can give the blocker a very powerful edge.

I don't think that the need for a very, very quick thrust at the moment of the snap is emphasized enough in youth football. You can correct this by talking about it. If he understands the concept and the edge it provides, he will have discovered a powerful tool. I remember thinking about trying to hit my opponent across the line before he even moved a muscle. Tell your player to consider this and to try it during practice. This approach will increase his quickness and add to the explosiveness of his initial contact. Even if the opponent is farther away, such as a linebacker or someone in the defensive backfield, a quick move is important. Quickness can be practiced!

Drive forward with the back foot. The back foot is the power foot, giving the body its thrust and forward momentum. Sure, both feet are used, but the back foot drives the body in the initial direction desired. It's good for a player just to be *aware* of where his power side is. This helps him draw from it.

Stay low, legs wide, knees bent. The most common mistake young linemen make, especially at the beginner level, is to stand up as the ball is hiked. This reduces the power of the forward thrust and eliminates any chance of delivering a good hard jolt to the opponent. The edge from knowing when the ball will be snapped is also lost, and the blocker becomes vulnerable. All he has is his strength, and the opponent now has an edge since defenders can fully use their hands to shed and shove the blocker sideways. A lineman must stay low with the charge and keep his head up and knees driving forward to build up maximum momentum.

Forearms rising forward, elbows out. The forearms are aimed for a point under the shoulders, rising forward in anticipation of contact, ready to slam into and raise the opponent's upper body upon contact. The elbows are initially out to broaden the blocker's breadth as much as possible. This helps to hinder the opponent who tries to shoot or dive by to one side or the other.

Angle, don't step, to the opponent's side. A common mistake blockers make is to initially step to one side, trying to cut off the opponent from the path of the ballcarrier. It's a natural move, and I did it myself plenty of times to secure an angle I needed. However, it reduces the momentum of the forward thrust and also lessens the edge obtained from knowing when the ball will be snapped. Overall, it takes away from the jolt that can be delivered. It's a trade-off. If I was stronger than my opponent, I preferred to secure the lane and didn't need the jolt since I could still overpower him. But if he was good, then I had to rely more on quickness.

Generally, the charge should be straight forward, angled just enough for the blocker to get his head on the side of the opponent where the ballcarrier will run. As noted below, the objective is to give the maximum jolt, and then, only after stunning the opponent, to try to turn and force him away from the play.

Detect and adjust for stunts. Again, if the charge is quick enough, a blocker can pop an opponent before he gets in gear. However, the blocker needs to pick up stunts and adjust accordingly, particularly if the opponent is not close. If the opponent is slanting to one side, then the blocker must adjust the thrust. If the opponent is a linebacker, then his stunt may take him out of the play and someone else will need to be blocked. Decisions must be made quickly, and the ability to adjust takes experience. It is important, however, to know which angle the opponent is taking, and to be generally aware of the surrounding traffic.

The Blocking Jolt

I love this word! It really captures the essence of what the blocker should try to do. Ask a player to think about what happens to him when he is jolted himself, how he feels stunned for a moment. Ask him how easy it would then be to move him around. This is how a blocker wants the opponent to feel, even if he is distracted for only a split second. A good jolt deflates the opponent's momentum and allows the blocker to stand him up and get deeper into his midsection. Furthermore, it distracts the tackler from finding the ballcarrier and, most important, teaches him respect for his blocker and makes him more cautious for future plays.

Jolt hard, as low as possible. If the opponent is head on or just to one side of the blocker, the jolt is the culmination of the charge. The basic idea is to slam a forearm and shoulder into the opponent as hard as possible. Sure, the blocker wants to be as low as possible and wants to get under the opponent's shoulder. But in close quarters, with only a split second, he has to take what he gets. He shouldn't sacrifice the jolt for position. A good jolt is a powerful and effective weapon. He can smash the forearm and shoulder into the opponent, then worry about what to do next. The ideal is to hit the opponent's upper thigh and drive up into the midsection. But, whatever part of the opponent he hits—often it's the shoulder—the objective is to belt it hard. The concept is to view the shoulder as a battering ram or as a boxer's punch, and throw it hard into the opponent. If the opponent is farther away, the blocker has time to dip just before making contact. The dip is like a windup that loads up more power, and it also serves to get the body a bit lower before the jolt.

Drive, don't lunge. The idea is to thrust and bring the back leg up. The initial charge is hard, but it is not a lunge. The knees straighten out upon contact. It's important to be under control so that the next move—a sustained block—can be carried out. The eyes must be open. The blocker must not turn his head away, for it is possible for the opponent to slide past him. The jolt occurs quickly, and a blocker needs to be under enough control to maintain balance and sustain contact with the defender.

Maintain balance. Often blockers lunge too hard, or the defender's quick reaction causes a blocker to make contact off-center. Whatever happens, it is critical to keep the legs wide and regain balance by bringing the back leg forward and under the body. The eyes must be open to assist with balance. The blocker leans directly into the defender's pressure. At all costs, he must avoid losing balance and falling to the ground. It happens too often, and a player can do little on the ground. If necessary, a block can be sustained by supporting the upper body with a hand on the ground. If the blocker does fall, he must keep blocking from the ground, sliding or crawling into the defender to try to interfere with the tackle in some way.

Drive up into the opponent with short, choppy steps and turn him. Once the jolt is delivered, with the legs still wide, the blocker drives the defender back with short, quick, choppy steps. He maneuvers his the body between the ballcarrier and the defender, lifting the defender with the hands and forearms. He keeps up constant pressure to interfere with the tackle, trying to turn the defender away from the path of the ballcarrier and then back to the line of scrimmage to prevent pursuit, and keeps his legs under his body as much as possible to avoid losing balance.

Use the hands, palms out, to shove the defender. One of the most common errors committed by an offensive lineman is holding. This is called as often as offside. A defender starts to get by a blocker and the blocker grabs him or wraps an arm around him. The blocker can use open hands, palms out, after delivering the jolt to push the defender, as long as his hands are extended and are out in front of the blocker's and opponent's frames. But he can't grab and he can't hold. Holding incurs a costly ten-yard penalty.

Specialty Blocks

Trap or mousetrap. It's a lot easier to block a player from the side than it is to block head on. Blocking from the side lets a blocker avoid all of the opponent's thrust and momentum. Therefore, traps are often set up. The simplest trap is a cross-block, in which two blockers who are next to each other cross and block each other's man. Usually the offensive tackle crosses in front of the offensive guard, and then the guard traps the defensive tackle from the side as he crosses the line of scrimmage. The offensive tackle must move out very quickly toward his man and thus get out of the guard's way. The guard pauses and then quickly pivots, charging with strength into the side of the onrushing defensive tackle. This works best when the defender is penetrating quickly, since the blocker can just "ride" him using his momentum and push him out of the path of the ball.

In other traps, a lineman pulls to trap a player. Usually a guard does the pulling, although occasionally a tackle pulls. The target of the trap can be the noseguard or perhaps a defensive end. When pulling, the blocker pushes to the side with his down hand, pivots, takes a small step with the back foot, and drives along the line of scrimmage with the front foot. Of course, this assumes that the back foot is on the same side he is pulling to. The arms pump quickly to get up speed. He must stay close to the line of scrimmage, dip by bending the knees, and with his eyes on the hip of the opponent, dip and give a jolt. If the pulling guard is to lead a play through a hole, he enters the hole, widens the legs, stays low, and anticipates the first defender to come from the inside (usually a linebacker).

If a guard with the right foot back has to pull to the left, then his first step is obviously with the left foot. Again the step is a short one and should be back a bit so as not to be too close to the line of scrimmage.

Sometimes the defender senses that a trap is coming, and he has been coached to drop immediately to all fours. If this occurs then the trapper must prepare to dig him out by driving into his side or shoulders and trying to turn him or just smother him. (See Figure 9.) The blocker must always play the defender, timing the charge to the speed and height of the defender.

Quickness is key. When blocking a player downfield, the first job is to get to the opponent as quickly as possible. This means the blocker must stay on his feet and must stay under enough control to make contact, so a shoulder block is preferable.

The blocker must know the path of the ballcarrier. Often a defensive back is approaching the ballcarrier at an angle. The blocker's objective is to get his head between the defensive back and the ballcarrier, step in front of the defender with the foot nearest the ballcarrier, and drive the opposite shoulder into the defender's midsection. In other words, if the runner is to the right and heading around right end, and the defensive back is approaching from the left, the blocker steps in front of the defender with his right foot and drives into him with the left shoulder. Once the blocker makes contact, he rides the defender and simply interferes, slowing him down as much as possible.

A well-timed *cross-body block* can also be effective. Here the player pivots on one foot, lifts the other leg outward, and turns his body horizontally, driving his hip into the opponent's midsection. Another option is the *crab block*, in which the blocker starts with a cross-body block and as he drops to the ground he crab-walks on all fours against the defender's legs.

The double-team is often used against a very strong defender. Two blockers simply drive their shoulders into either side of the opponent and drive him back. Another option is the *post and*

FIGURE 9
DIG HIM OUT

The defenseman has dropped to all fours so the blocker comes in low to dig him out.

wheel, in which one blocker hits head on and the other hits to one side, trying to turn the defender away. (See Figure 10.)

Finally, pass blocking. Here the blocker does not charge, but drops back a step and holds his ground. His feet are churning, and his responsibility is to block the area he is standing in. The blocker lets the defender come to him! He looks to pick up any stunts and he jolts the first defender to approach. He keeps his hands in front and his legs churning. The idea is to interfere with and stop the pass rusher, or at least to slow down or turn the defender to the outside. The best technique is to *shiver blow.* Drive both palms forward and up into the defender's shoulders, then recoil and shiver again.

Pass blocking is much easier than other types of blocking, as long as the blocker keeps his balance, stays on his feet, and interferes with the pass rusher for as long as possible. The objective here is not to overcome the rusher; it is to slow him down and thus protect the passer.

Other blockers. The focus to this point has been on blocking by linemen. Many of these techniques apply as well to blocking by running backs. They often find themselves facing a situation similar to that of a downfield blocker. On a sweep play, the blocking back needs to get outside the defender if he can. On a play to the right, he must get the right foot out in front of the defender and squeeze the left hand and elbow in front of him also. Then he simply drives into the defender with the left shoulder. This kind of open field block form is also useful for guards when they pull on ends and is similar to downfield blocking form. If the play is designed to cut inside, then the blocker reverses and hits with the outside shoulder, driving the defender outside.

TACKLING

I believe tackling is the act that best demonstrates the essence of football. The most tenacious kids on the team will play defense; they will do so because they make tackles. Tackles don't have to be pretty, they just need to stop the ball. Less aggressive kids can play the offensive line, but defensive play absolutely demands de-

FIGURE 10

POST AND WHEEL

One blocker (the post) hits from the front and the other wheels the tackler around from the side.

sire and the kid who loves the fray. Good tacklers are hard, tough kids.

Tackling is the act of stopping the forward progress of the ball by forcing the ballcarrier to the ground. The object is to stop the ball cold, not even allowing the running back to fall forward. The ideal tackle hits the ballcarrier hard enough to force him backward, preferably causing him to lose possession of the ball. A fine crunching tackle always brings great praise from fans, coach and teammates.

Proper form for tackling comes naturally to an aggressive kid. His mind is focused on stopping the ballcarrier, and anyone else is just an obstacle to be overcome quickly. He claws and fights by or through the interference and comes in hard on the running back. There are, however, several concepts and techniques that the beginner should understand.

I will discuss defense in general and the play of individual defensive positions in later chapters.

The Defensive Line Stance

Every single play in football begins with a proper stance. This holds true for each player—offense and defense, linemen, backs and receivers. Everyone should start each play with a proper stance. Tackling, therefore, also begins with a solid stance, especially for the down linemen. The worst thing for a defender to do (besides getting knocked down) is to allow a blocker to get a shoulder into his belly. The defensive stance is less rigid than the offensive stance, since an offensive lineman cannot move once he is set. Defenders can adjust, stunt or change the intended angle of thrust at any time, depending on the situation.

Defensive stance. The defensive down lineman's stance is similar to the blocker's. Feet are wide and balanced; weight is moderately forward but significantly more forward than the blocker's; and the back is straight, with the tail down. (See Figure 11.) The defensive lineman must stay close to, but not in, the neutral zone.

As low as possible. The lineman's shoulder should be even with or lower than the blocker's shoulder. As stated before, the

FIGURE 11

DEFENSIVE STANCE
Low, similar to a
blocker, but weight is
more forward for
more thrust.

worst thing a lineman can do is rise up too quickly and let the
blocker give a blow to his midsection. I find a three-point stance,
with the weight balanced, to be somewhat preferable. A four-point
stance may be used, particularly by shorter, quicker players. If a
four-point stance is used, the weight should be distributed evenly
on all fours.

One foot back, preferably the inside foot. Since the down
lineman can more squarely handle an outside blocker on a sweep
or off-tackle run if he brings up his inside foot first, it is better for
the down lineman to keep his inside foot back a bit. The ankles
can be flared out a bit for more power.

Eyes forward, searching for clues. Defensive linemen check
their opponent's eyes and look for any slight lean by the opponent.
They look at the quarterback, running backs and other linemen,
trying to get a feel for the direction of the play. They should think
about the down and the yardage, and whether a pass or a run is
likely. Usually teams won't run the same play twice, so a good
defender thinks where they might choose to go next. Valuable clues
can be gained. But a defensive lineman must not think so much
that he forgets to watch the snap or fails to react to what actually
occurs.

Crouch stance. Standing defensemen like ends and linebackers stand in a crouch, knees slightly bent, inside foot forward, arms hanging to the side, hands waist high, palms out, and weight forward on the balls of the feet.

Tackling Techniques

A number of phrases are used for the first defensive move. The basic idea is to meet the blocker, neutralize his charge, and move into the pressure to find and stop the ballcarrier. It is critical to keep these first two concepts in mind: The tackler must hit the blocker to neutralize him, then recover and shed the blocker.

Common errors are rising too soon to look for the ballcarrier, and trying to shed the blocker by stepping around him without neutralizing the charge. A tackler must give the blocker a good jolt of his own. Keep repeating: Hit and hunt, shiver and shed, neutralize and move on. Let's go through these steps one by one.

Watch the snap and move quickly upon it. The defense is not allowed to be in or across the neutral zone when the ball is snapped (although defenders may retreat back across the line before the ball is snapped as long as they make no contact while offside). Defenders must anticipate the snap and explode very quickly upon it. The first move in football is almost always the most important, and quickness is usually behind most successful moves. The quarterback will try to pull linemen offside by varying his cadence, and referees will allow him to do so unless it is flagrant. So, while players must listen to the cadence, and tense up near the time for the snap, it is the snap that must be focused upon. The offense knows the count. They have the clear advantage of surprise and so can build up momentum behind their charge and jolt. The defender can compensate for some of this by using quickness to minimize the offensive momentum. (See Figure 12.)

Neutralize the blocker's charge. There are basically two ways to do this: a shoulder charge and a shiver charge. A shoulder charge is used when the idea is to penetrate the defense. The defender jolts the shoulder against or under the blocker's shoulder just like in a block, then brings up the forearms to lift the opponent,

FIGURE 12

CHARGE

This tackler (see arrow) has mounted a fine charge and is bringing arms forward and up to the blocker's chest.

brings up the back foot for balance, and drives through using short, choppy steps. He must always have his head up, looking for the flow and pressure and searching for the running back. The key is to stop the blocker's charge and momentum and thus be in better shape to shed him. A shoulder charge can also be used when no penetration is desired, such as a short yardage situation when the defense needs to protect territory. In this case, the defender focuses more on neutralizing and then on *lifting* the blocker.

The shiver is used to protect territory by neutralizing and holding the blocker at bay while looking for the ball. (See Figure 13.) Defensive ends and linebackers use it most, but it can also be used by down linemen who want to mix up their approaches. The idea is to jam the opponent's shoulder pad in an upward direction with a stiff straight-arm move, palms out, using both hands. The lineman keeps the opponent away until he spots the ballcarrier and then sheds him. Again, neutralizing the blocker's charge head-on is almost always preferable to trying to step around him, since such avoidance moves often expose a player to an easy block from the side. Another common error is to rise to look for the ball before neutralizing the blocker.

Sometimes a neutralizing charge is not used, such as in a *submarine dive*, a knee-high dive between two opponents during which the defender uses his quickness to penetrate. The key here is to bring the legs up very quickly and do a push-up with the arms to

FIGURE 13

SHIVER

This defender neutralizes the blocker with a shiver, holds him at bay, and prepares to shed him.

regain a ready position after diving through the line. It works well against taller blockers or blockers who don't stay low. Another quickness play is to dive over the top of a very low blocker, arms extended to break the fall, landing on bent legs, crouched and ready to drive. These moves are used particularly by the noseguard to mix up his stunts and keep the blocker off-balance. However, a hard neutralizing charge is usually the best way to control the neutral zone and win ball games.

Stay under control. If no blocker shows up, there is no one to neutralize. When a defensive lineman doesn't get blocked immediately, chances are someone is pulling from the line and preparing to trap him from the side. Bells should go off! He should slow down, stay under control, drop to the ground, give the trap blocker a forearm or a shoulder, hold fast and stack things up. He can scratch and crawl on all fours toward the ballcarrier, trying to slow him down or stop him. If he only plugs up the hole, he at least forces the runner to go around him—hopefully closer to another defender.

Recover and shed. When both players receive a jolt, chances are the defender got hit harder due to the blocker's greater momentum. This is why the recovery must start simultaneously with the jolt. To recover, the lineman brings the forearms up, lifts and begins to push the opponent away, and drives forward with short, choppy steps. He looks for the ball and drives toward it. (See Figure 14.)

Focus and wrap. Now it's showtime—it's just your tackler and the running back. Once he has thrust the blocker to one side, he should drop back to a low position, keep moving, and focus on the runner's belt. (See Figure 15.) He spreads his feet and drives his shoulder into the midsection or upper leg area. He jolts with the shoulder, brings his legs up quickly and his hands together, and clasps his arms tightly around the runner. He then lifts and drops him quickly.

Sometimes in a running situation, a side tackle, an ankle tackle, a tackle from behind, or a tackle falling in front of the runner is all that is available. The defender should try to get a shoulder into the runner, but he can't be choosy. He must muscle the runner down any way possible—but remember to focus, jolt, and wrap the arms when possible. (See Figure 16.)

When rushing a passer, the defender should get the arms high, waving them to obstruct vision or block the pass, then bring the arms crashing down upon the passer from above, wrapping the arms and hugging the passer to the ground.

PASSING

By the turn of the twentieth century, football was perceived as a brutal and dangerous game. President Teddy Roosevelt insisted that the recently organized NCAA legalize the forward pass, and this probably saved the game. Modern footballs are slimmer to facilitate the passing game.

Quarterbacks do much more than pass, and they require a rare combination of talents. However, to pass they should preferably be tall and have big hands, strong arms, good eyes, full field vision, courage, a knack for knowing when to release the ball, and, of course, throwing accuracy.

In the grade school level there are far fewer passes than later on at the high school level. The pros nowadays pass about half of the time, but each youth team runs maybe thirty-five to forty plays a game and throws the ball only a few times. Passing is the most complicated thing in football. A lot can go wrong, and interceptions

FIGURE 14
SHED
Hold the opponent at bay with arms out and shed to go for the ballcarrier at the right moment. Here #61 sheds #74 to tackle #21.

FIGURE 15
Focus on the belt. Attack low.

FIGURE 16
Stay low. Get shoulder into the runner.

occur often at youth levels. Turnovers are a heavy price to pay and coaches worry about putting the ball up too much. I believe much of the problem comes from lack of proper form with the quarterback. A young quarterback is nervous, excited and inexperienced, and the first thing that goes under pressure is form. I doubt that youth coaches emphasize form enough. They seem to rely too much on the natural ability of their passer.

Learning some essentials of passing form creates a solid foundation for a young quarterback, and that greatly adds to his passing accuracy. If you practice these essentials you will soon notice a difference in his poise, confidence and success. The mechanics of passing are not difficult, but they must be practiced enough so that they become automatic. From such a foundation of strength and stability your quarterback can perform at a higher level. I'll discuss pass patterns in chapter five.

Snap and Retreat

Think! A pass play begins as soon as the quarterback breaks the huddle. He sizes up the defense. His gaze must be impassive, always starting from the same side of the field and slowly sweeping and scanning the secondary. Can he spot a blitz? Is a defender out of position? Where are the seams? Where will there be a height mismatch? Has the wind changed and does it favor a long or short pass? How do things "feel"?

Take the snap comfortably. The quarterback's hands should be firmly pressed against the center's crotch, firmly enough so that the center clearly knows exactly where they are. The passing hand is on top, other hand on the bottom. The insides of the wrists are touching with the fingers spread (some rotate the hand a bit so that the thumbs are up more—each quarterback should do what's comfortable). The key is to take the snap securely and quickly. (See Figure 17.)

Retreat quickly. A right-handed player quickly turns to the right, pushes off with the left foot, and steps back with the right foot. Sometimes he fakes a handoff to slow down the defensive charge. Some quarterbacks simply backpedal the entire 4 to 6 yards.

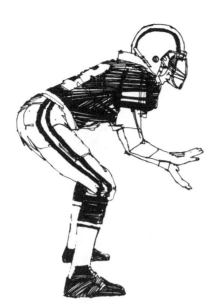

FIGURE 17
SNAP POSITION
The quarterback's form
here is excellent: low,
poised and balanced.

Although this provides a clearer view of the secondary, there is a
chance of tripping. Whatever method is used, the idea is to get back
very quickly so there is time to pick up the downfield action. The
snap, the footwork, the pivot, the quick drop-back, and the number
of steps taken should be practiced repeatedly. The passer's hands
should be kept high at the end of the retreat.

Quick-outs (passes to the flat) or quick slant passes may require
only one to three steps. Most other passes require five steps, always
starting and ending with the right (back) foot if the quarterback is
right-handed. A quarterback must practice these steps and make
them routine. Fumbles or missteps occur often, and they can turn
a whole game around. It must all be automatic, so that in a game
situation the passer can focus more on his primary receiver and on
the reaction of the defensive secondary.

Step forward. Once the passer takes the prescribed number of
steps backward, he should stop, pause, and then take a step forward. The outside pass rusher will angle on the back point of his
drop, so the final step forward into the "pocket" affords more protection. Of course, if there is a weakness up the middle and pressure

comes from there, adjustments must be made. The quarterback may need to roll out to the flat to buy more time. He must stay cool, not panic and focus downfield, so he can get the pass off, not recklessly or in desperation, but under control. And remember, a sack is always better than an interception.

Grip the ball, hands up at the shoulder. In the normal retreat the quarterback should hold the ball up even with the shoulder by the side of his head, using a proper passing grip in the throwing hand and protecting the ball with the other hand. The left or free hand should be kept on the ball, protecting it until ready to release it. This is a good habit; developing it early will definitely save an occasional fumble. The ball should be gripped snugly, not squeezed, with the fingers spread wide and touching the ball along their entire length. The hand grips it in back of center, with the pinky near the middle of the ball. The laces are under the last joints of the fingers. Some space should exist between the side of the palm and the ball. Again, comfort is desirable. A wide finger spread is the best, but, of course, large hands are needed for that. Special exercises to stretch the fingers backward and sideways can improve the grip and should be done. (See Figure 18.)

The Pass Release
Survey, stand erect, hold the ball high, and step to the receiver. Okay, now for the moment of truth. The first job is to decide who gets the ball. Usually, that's already planned by the play pattern called in the huddle. The pattern will send two or three receivers into the defensive secondary and is designed so that the *primary* receiver winds up with only individual coverage, one-on-one. Even the timing of the throw is sometimes predetermined so the passer knows about when the receiver will break to one side, or speed up and go deep. The idea usually is to hit the receiver just after he breaks to one side, since that is when the defender is farthest from him, particularly if the receiver has faked convincingly to the other side.

Passers usually try to hit a receiver as he moves from one defensive zone to another, since he is most "open" when he is in the

FIGURE 18
Retreat with the ball high, protect it with the
free hand, and look at developing pass patterns.
Grip the laces under tip joints of fingers.

seam between defenders. However, the passer needs to be flexible
enough to know how far the defender is from his primary receiver,
to see if another defender is double-teaming his primary, and perhaps then to take a peek at his secondary receiver. For all of this,
the passer has only a second or two. He must stand erect to get the
fullest possible view, legs comfortable but not spread apart too
much. His weight is on the back—usually the right—foot. The quarterback holds the ball high and then steps toward his target, toward
where the receiver should be when the ball arrives. Taking too big
a step causes a late release and an underthrown pass. A half yard
is fine—just a moderate step.

Snap the wrist. On a long pass, the nose of the ball should tilt
up a bit so that it floats and settles safely into the receiver's hands.
Of course, the farther the pass, the more the passer needs to lead

the receiver. If there is to be a mistake on a long pass, it is better to err by overthrowing. The passer's arm must move straight as his weight is shifted to the front foot. His free arm is extended, preferably in the direction of the pass. The forward arm movement is very quick and snaps the wrist in a whipping motion, rolling the ball off the fingers, little finger first. The wrist snap causes the ball to spiral evenly, and a nice spiral is easier to catch. The wrist brings the hand and fingers downward and inward as the ball rolls away. The spin need not, and should not, be too fast—just moderate.

A short pass needs an even harder wrist snap. It must be fired very hard since the ball must quickly thread its way through several outreaching defensive hands. It's usually better to underthrow a short pass if an error is to be made, since there usually are more defenders deep. The nose of the ball should be level or even down a hair, and the passer should follow through fully.

Jump passes. Quarterbacks often have to throw passes while on the run. Initially the quarterback holds the ball to his side to hide it. Then, he raises and holds the ball high, faking the release, if possible, to slow a charging defender or perhaps get him to jump. If the secondary drops back, a run may be possible. Otherwise the quarterback should throw, remembering that less of a lead is needed if the receiver is moving in the same direction (to compensate for the passer's own momentum). If the passer must jump to get more strength on the pass or to avoid a defender, he should release the ball with a quick wrist snap at the top of the jump. Taking the final step a bit forward, if possible, helps get some momentum on the ball.

Drills

The ideal pass is about 10 to 15 yards long, so these should be practiced the most. Rest the arm on alternate days. Tell parents to remember that their son is throwing in practice, so their assistance is best during the off-season, or during times when he has not been throwing too much. Do about twenty to thirty passes, going in and out, across the middle, quick short passes. Don't wear out his arm with too many long bombs, and save them for the end of practice when you are sure he has loosened up plenty.

Have him practice with a wet ball. It will rain sometimes, and experience with a wet ball is very useful on such days. It's sometimes necessary to face the palm out more to maintain grip and contact on a wet ball for short passes. Let him attempt different approaches to find what works best. He should also pass off-balance in practice. I don't know why coaches don't practice it, but it does happen in games and that is what practice is for—to help execute better under game conditions. The hardest pass is when fading backward (and probably should not be thrown), but practice it anyway.

RECEIVING

Nothing gets a crowd going like the reception of a long, beautiful pass. Receivers, especially wide receivers, have become a rare breed. They are agile athletes, preferably tall, are great leapers, have speed, and play with enormous courage. No one gets hit as hard as a receiver coming down with his full weight into a helmet or shoulder of a tough defender.

You don't see many passes at the younger youth levels. Coaches know that the 50 percent completion rate in the Pros is many times higher than that for nine- to thirteen-year-old kids. Interceptions are common at young ages. Again, this is an area where kids don't get a lot of work. Unfortunately, in most states, as with many youth sports, there are limits to the amount of practice kids get. In my hometown, the kids practice only twice a week during the season. Some leagues limit the number of practice hours. Also, many towns have no lights for evening practice, although more and more now have them.

Here are some definite guidelines for receivers to follow.

Get off the line. I haven't seen many youth teams that check or delay the offensive end or wide receiver at the line of scrimmage. The idea is to delay the receiver so the passer has less time to pass. This move is more common in high school, perhaps because more passes are thrown at older ages. In any event, if someone tries to delay your player he must know that a quick fake step to one side, with arms out front, and perhaps a "shiver and shed" move will be needed. Sometimes, just a blast of speed around the defender is sufficient.

Run directly at the defender. This is a crucial first move. The natural impulse is to angle away from the defender, but that removes the ability to fake. The receiver should run hard right at the defender, as fast as possible, as if to run right through him. This takes away the defender's chance to anticipate the receiver's ultimate direction, and it should help to get him a bit off-balance.

Make the move just as the defender commits. Once the defender starts retreating, fully committed and backpedaling sufficiently, then the receiver should put on the next move. This means the receiver needs to concentrate on the defender's momentum. (See Figure 19.) If he is backpedaling quickly, a fake may not be needed; the receiver can just cut quickly and sharply according to the pass pattern. However, a fake usually helps, so the receiver should take two or three steps to one direction and then cut sharply to the other. A head fake or a one-step fake is often not enough. The second or third step will change the defender's momentum and spring the receiver loose for the pass. This requires moving quickly, but under control, particularly in the final steps of the pattern. There is no need for full speed and the receiver needs to save a bit to allow for a reaction to the pass—it may be short or long.

Don't forget your quarterback. The passer is under tremendous pressure and may need to unload early. How often does a pass fall near a receiver who never turned to see what was happening? The receiver must look to the passer as soon as he breaks from his fake. The receiver must forget the defender for a moment, and make eye contact with the passer as quickly as possible—he needs some attention immediately.

Focus, soft hands, wait for the ball. When the ball is up in the air, quick decisions have to be made. The receiver adjusts his speed to meet the ball. Eyes must be on the ball. The receiver must not reach for it until it gets close, since that can tip off the defender as to its timing. Often the defender turns his back on the ball and watches the receiver's body language to signal when it's time to turn for the ball. So, again, the receiver must not reach early, and must try to remain calm. The arms and hands should be relaxed, with soft fingers ready to receive the ball; the hands are gently withdrawn upon contact to soften the impact.

Catch it high, use the hands, fingers curled and spread. A pass should be caught as high as possible. First, this reduces the chance for an interception. Second, it gets the receiver off the ground. The body is smooth as it glides through the air, but it is bumpy while running; getting off the feet helps for a smooth catch.

The receiver should catch with the hands and curl the fingers. The fingers should curl into the form of the ball. If they are straight, the ball tends to bounce off the palm. Too often kids try to trap the ball with their arms. It's okay to use the chest and arms to trap the ball, but the hands are always more effective.

Try this tip and tell your player to try it: Focus on the front tip of the ball and try to catch it. It really helps to focus concentration and hand placement. Watching the ball all the way into the hands is critical. Tell him to watch the spin of the ball or try to see the laces spinning as he catches it. A receiver has a certain "oneness" with the ball. He should feel as though he has already caught it while it is still in the air.

In a deep pattern the receiver arches his back and raises his hands, palms back. On a buttonhook (see glossary) he faces the ball, hands in a W shape. On a pass across the middle the best place to catch the ball is just in front of the inside shoulder.

The receiver must catch and tuck the ball in before running. This may sound obvious, but kids often think about running before they secure the catch, or maybe they are bracing for an expected hit. The most important job for a receiver is to firmly catch and tuck the ball before doing anything else.

Change direction immediately. The defense tends to flow with the receiver's momentum and direction, so making an immediate change of direction after a reception is usually quite effective. The move is particularly recommended when the receiver does not know where the coverage is around him. This helps to break away for a few more yards, or perhaps spring a long run. A spin move also helps at this point. However, he must still remember that the most important thing is to have the ball tucked in securely.

Recover and tackle if intercepted. If the pass is intercepted, chances are the intended receiver has the best first shot at the tackle. He should recover immediately, not get mad at himself and not turn into a spectator. Now his job is to get the opponent and bring him down.

Drills

As with passing, the best receiving drill is just doing it. If your receiver is young you may wish to throw while down on one knee to simulate the height of the normal ball release of his quarterback. If there are a few kids around, set them up in a secondary and keep throwing. Have your checklist handy and keep calling out these helpful hints. It's good for him to practice catching passes with one hand. Throw to one side, then to the other. It helps to train the hands to react properly.

RUNNING

At the grade school level, football is a running game. The great majority of plays involve running the ball, and most yardage seems to be gained on wide running sweeps. Often the team with a real speedster breaks open big plays around the end for the score. Of course, plays are also run up the middle, but blocking techniques are usually not very well developed yet, and so defensive linemen and linebackers pretty much control the middle.

Most people seem to feel that the glory of football is found at the running back position. I guess over the years the Jim Browns and the Walter Paytons have gotten the most exposure. Anyone who has played football has great respect for all positions and knows that the fierce hand-to-hand combat in the middle of the line is really the heart and soul of the game. However, the running backs put the numbers up on the scoreboard. They get hit very hard and earn every bit of their attention. My son played fullback his first year, and while he didn't have great speed, he used to buck the line with a full and reckless abandon, dropping his shoulder and often giving a linebacker a shot of his own.

The Basics

The stance. The runner needs a stance from which he can move in any direction with ease and quickness. As with the linemen, runners start with a ready position—feet spread apart, hands on the knees and eyes straight ahead. Then they drop into a set position. Some coaches prefer them to stay up in ready position since this allows for a better read of the developing hole they must run through, but it sacrifices quickness.

Since most running plays, except for dives straight up the middle, require lateral movement, a runner must be able to move laterally very quickly. A spread and balanced foot position allows for a push to either side, so in the set position a runner's legs are fairly wide apart. One foot, usually the inside foot, is set back, but only a few inches behind the front. Again, this helps balance. The hand on the same side as the back foot is straight down, but not much weight is on it. It is mainly for balance. The head is up and the back straight like a lineman's. The body is tense, coiled and ready to spring. The toes are straight ahead, or even pointed outward a bit since the push comes from the inside front or balls of the feet. (See Figure 20.)

It is essential to get into exactly the same stance every play. The defense is looking intently for a clue as to where the play will go.

FIGURE 19
Make the cut sharply (as done here by #23) and quickly look toward the passer.

FIGURE 20
RUNNING BACK STANCE

The two deep backs have legs spread ready to move laterally, with little weight forward. The fullback, however, has a lot of weight forward since he is going straight ahead (and perhaps tipping off the play).

The running backs must not help them out by leaning or looking to the side where the play will go. Head, shoulders and eyes are forward and impassive.

Pivot and snap. As I watch pre-high-school games, I am struck by how long it takes for the backfield action to develop. The problem is often that the running back gets to the hole too late. A blocker gives a jolt, as described earlier, and attempts to sustain the block, but the defender can use his hands freely to shed him. Therefore, the running back must get there before the defender fully recovers. A split second makes all the difference, especially at young ages when sustained blocking is the exception and not the rule. The four or five yards between the running back and the line of scrimmage are critical. Getting there quickly is more important than what happens later. In fact, the first move, the pivot and snap, is the most important of all.

Running backs must fully pivot toward their intended direction before they ever take a step. They snap the head and shoulders in that direction, shifting weight by pushing off the ball of the foot opposite to that direction. Only *after* the pivot do they take the first, large step, with the foot closest to the intended direction. Stepping first just wastes time. It is much quicker to pivot first and then step out directly. This technique must be practiced until it is automatic. The head and shoulder snap adds to the overall quickness of the move. The idea is to take off low, stay low, and then build up speed with strong churning arm movement.

Look at the hole; receive the handoff securely. A running back should not worry about the quarterback. The quarterback's job is to get the ball to the runner safely. The runner must look at the gap he will run through. He scrutinizes the area to see what is developing and to see whether a key block will be successful.

The quarterback should present the ball firmly, usually with one hand on the outside and underside of the ball, well into the runner's midsection, just above the belt. The quarterback must focus squarely on the runner's belt. When the play is into the middle of the line, the runner receives the ball with his far arm relaxed down in front of the opposite hip, palm toward the ball, and the elbow and forearm nearest the quarterback raised chest high, ready to help cover and secure the ball. He then curls both hands around the opposite tips of the ball, covering the tips—not just circling them. On a wide play the runner may receive the ball in the midsection, or he may take it with the hands, depending on the speed and motion needed.

Carry the ball securely. Most fumbles do not occur because of a powerful defensive jolt, but because the ball was not carried securely. In one game my son's team, a very strong team, lost the ball on the first play of their first two possessions because the same running back carried the ball through the line like it was a flag, waving it around wildly.

The proper carrying technique is to jam the point of the ball into the pocket between the upper arm and ribs, just below the armpit. The forearm is stretched along the side of the ball, slightly to the underside. The upper hand is curled around the front tip, fingers spread to the inside. The technique is designed to protect the ball, and every protection is needed. Tacklers not only hit hard, they are

FIGURE 21
RUNNING BACKS
Secure the ball snugly in the armpit.

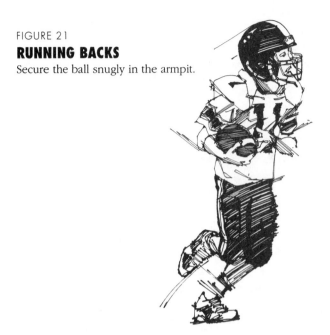

instructed to try to tear or slash the ball free, especially the second tackler on the scene. (See Figure 21.)

The ball is carried in the right arm when running right and in the left arm when running left. When running in the open field, the runner may switch hands to get the ball away from the nearest approaching tackler, but only if he is absolutely sure there is time. He must make sure the new hand has the ball before sliding it across the midsection for the switch.

Run with power, run hard, and give a second effort. Now it's time to get yardage. The single focus of the running back must be to get as much yardage as possible. He doesn't worry about the tackler; he looks mainly for daylight. When a tackler appears, he continues to run hard—to get that precious yardage. A good running back avoids the tackler's shoulder, runs right through his arms, twists, turns, and keeps his legs underneath with short, driving steps. He falls forward or lunges for the extra few inches. One of the truly beautiful phrases in football is *second effort*. This concept and determination to fight through contact will drive the good running back to gain much more yardage.

Straight-arm and other maneuvers. I don't see the *straight-*

arm too much anymore, yet it is a most useful weapon against the tackle. This idea is to reach out just as the tackler lunges, place the palm out onto his shoulder or helmet, then point the shoulder at him and firmly straighten out and lock the arm. The runner must not give the arm too early or the tackler will avoid (or grab) it. As soon as his arm makes contact, the runner should leap a bit. This substantially reduces the tackler's jolt and can catapult the runner a few yards. A stiff arm can also be effective to push the tackler down or away, particularly if he is off-balance.

Another move is the *step-out*, in which the runner jabs a sharp step toward the tackler to get him to tense up and then pushes off laterally away from him, perhaps with a straight-arm. The runner can also pivot from a jab step by merely swinging the other foot around in a full 360-degree turn away from the defender's momentum.

The *crossover* is a third avoidance measure in which the leg nearest the tackler is lifted high and away as the body also leans away. This is usually effective on a sweep or wide play before the defender gets too close.

Even though maneuvers such as the straight-arm, step-out and crossover can be useful, most often the runner bucks the line on a dive or off-tackle run, keeping the body low and looking for just one more inch.

SPECIALTIES

I'll discuss special teams more a bit later when I review the overall strategy of offense and defense. Special teams are used for kicking, primarily for kickoffs, field goals, points after touchdown and punts. As you can see, these teams are on the field mainly when possession is being formally transferred to the opponent (kickoff and punt) or when attempting to score by placekicking (field goal and point after touchdown). The action is often spread over the entire field with players running at full speed. There are some very special and quite important skills involved, particularly kicking skills, and players should seriously consider developing them. From nine to thirteen years old the kicks in the kickoff normally range from 20 to 40 yards, increasing about 4 to 5 yards each year. More often than not the ball is miskicked and travels close to the ground, bouncing after 15 yards. Have your players try punting and placekicking, particularly if any have played soccer. Good kickers are very rare and very valuable to grade school teams, and with a bit of practice it is incredible how quickly a youngster can improve. Most kids just never try it. Other specialties such as catching punts and kickoffs and hiking the snaps for kickers are also important.

The Snap

In the Pros, the punter lines up 12 to 15 yards behind the line of scrimmage. At youth levels it is 7 to 10 yards, and that's still quite a hike for a young center. The field goal or point after touchdown (PAT) snap is a few yards shorter, although placekicks are still quite rare at the youth level. The center should practice the snap regularly, preferably with the team's actual punter or placekick holder. The snap is similar to an upside down pass: the harder and faster, the better. A fast snap can save a precious split second and avoid a blocked punt.

The center should get into a normal stance, with the back foot a bit farther back if that is more comfortable. He then raises the front point of the ball and places the right hand up near the front, similar to a passer's grip. His left hand is on the side of the ball to help guide it, particularly if his hands are small. The left hand leaves the ball first. Weight is moderately forward upon the ball, as is normal for snaps. Driving the ball back in a quick snapping motion, the center aims for the area between the punter's knee and waist, or directly to the hands of the placekick holder. He should give the ball as little arc as possible and make the snap hard. Finally, he must make sure that the snap is completed before worrying about the noseguard; the snap is more important than he is. Blocked punts are always a major disaster. Bracing and stepping forward with the snap for balance helps avoid bad snaps.

Punting

Punting is often avoided at the very young ages unless *very* long yardage is needed for a first down, or the team is backed up very near their own goal line. The potential for disaster is quite high. A bad snap, poor blocking, a slow punter all combine to discourage coaches from trying it, particularly when the successful kick often gains only 10 to 15 yards. Coaches figure the heck with it. They take their chances with a sweep around the end and hope to get lucky.

Before the ball is snapped, the punter surveys the plant area in front of him to ensure that there is good footing. He then looks only at the ball. (See Figure 22.) His feet are parallel. His weight is on the left foot if he is a righty. The arms are extended outward, palms down and inward, thumbs up, fingers spread and curled a bit. He stands erect, hands soft, body relaxed.

Now he concentrates and lets the ball come all the way to his hands. The hands should withdraw slightly to soften contact. He places the laces up, and the right hand is back a bit, cradling the ball. Take a short step with the kicking foot and a second longer and quicker step with the other foot, planting it firmly and securely.

FIGURE 22
PUNTING FORM
Punts are often avoided at youth levels. Practice here can make a player a rare and valuable asset.

Extending and serving the ball over the kicking leg with the front of the ball pointed downward a little and turned slightly to the inside, the punter places the ball on his foot with the right hand. He must not "drop" it too far; the less distance it travels the better.

The kick will spiral if the ball is kicked with the outside of the instep, with the right side of the shoelaces contacting the underbelly of the ball. It will travel end over end if kicked on the instep squarely along the bottom seam of the ball. The knee at first is relaxed. As it comes forward, it whips the rigidly locked ankle forward in a hard snapping motion to give power and distance to the punt. The foot comes forward in a smooth pendulum motion, not sideways, and follows through to shoulder height at least, pulling the body forward in a hopping motion. The left arm may raise up and swing across the chest to help balance and torque.

The punter only has a couple of seconds to do all of this. He must be quick, balanced and under control. Good practice drills

FIGURE 23
Receive punts with the hands and then bring into the body.

have the punter kick about 5 to 10 yards, to a teammate (or to a parent) slowly, watching the form and point of contact with the ball, trying to lay the ball on the instep with as little extra distance as possible. Have him tap it to you, and he should learn enough control so you don't have to move to catch it at all. Then, have him overcompensate the other way, booming kicks for maximum power and distance. He should try to get the kick away in about two seconds from the snap.

Catching Punts

The receiver should stand about 5 yards deeper than the punter can kick so he is moving forward as he receives the ball. This could add at least 5 yards to the return. The receiver should have his arms raised forward and upward a bit. Palms should be up, fingers spread, and hands fairly close together. The ball should always be caught with the hands and then brought into the midsection quickly for protection. The body and hands should withdraw, even squat a bit, to soften impact. (See Figure 23.)

Placekicking

Soccer-style kicking has pretty much taken over football. It gives just as much power and much more accuracy than the toe kicking of olden days. If a player has a good strong foot, try him at it. The kicker takes two or three steps, depending on the distance needed, in a quarter-circle motion. He measures the distance and stands with legs even, leaning forward a bit on the front foot. The holder kneels on the left knee near where he will place the ball, right leg extended forward, arms reaching toward the ball. He receives the snap, lowers the ball to the spot, turns the laces facing forward (out of the way of the foot), and places the end of the right hand exactly on the tip, removing the left hand. He looks only at the ball. It should be nearly straight up, tilted a hair backward, depending on the kicker's preference. The kicker takes the two or three steps and plants the free foot pointing straight at the target, toes even with the back of the ball and several inches to the side, depending on the kicker's comfort and style.

The kickoff is just a long placekick, except that the kicker takes numerous steps, covering at least 5 yards, and the ball is kicked off a tee. Otherwise, the techniques are the same. Kids can kick off at a range of 20 to 40 yards. If he can consistently deliver 30 plus yards by age ten, he could try out for this position.

Now that we've discussed the basic skills, let's see how they're used by each position.

Chapter Four

FIELD POSITIONS

WHAT POSITION SHOULD EACH CHILD PLAY?

Well, that's mainly up to the coach. During the first practice or two a coach usually asks kids to split up into positions of their own choice, but very quickly the coach determines where they play. The first wind sprints, 30 to 40 yard dashes, tell the coach where his speed is, and speed is the primary determinant separating backs and linemen. Usually, the coach has several rules of thumb; sometimes he must assign a person to a certain position just because there is no one else on the team who can play that position. Remember, football is a team sport, and each player must play where he is needed most.

In general, the fastest kids play in the *backfield* on both offense and defense. The biggest, most heavily built kids play on the *line*. Aggressive kids who combine speed, strength and agility play *linebacker*. Taller kids who have some quickness play *end*—offensive end if they can catch and block, defensive end if they can make tackles. In fact, if any kid has aggressiveness and can produce tackles, the coach will find him a place somewhere on *defense*. Big, strong, slower kids play *offensive line*, and the largest kids in this group play tackle. (See Figure 24.)

The quarterback is the one who has it all: brains to spare, a strong arm, and the ability to complete passes. He must be able to receive snaps, remember complex plays (not just his role, but everyone else's too), and hand off the ball securely.

Sure, coaches have favorites. Sometimes it does not seem fair who gets to play where. But a coach's main motivation is to succeed, and he should generally put kids where they fit best. A kid's attitude plays a large role too. The kid who has a bad attitude, who is oversensitive, or who demonstrates any sort of problem will be

FIGURE 24
FIELD POSITIONS

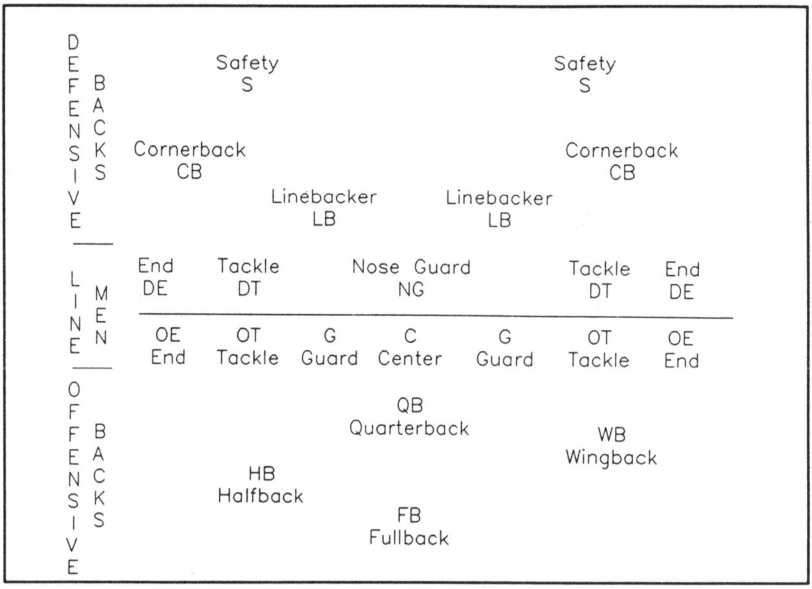

```
D
E
F              Safety                    Safety
E     B          S                         S
N     A
S     C
S     K   Cornerback                    Cornerback
I     S       CB                            CB
V
E                    Linebacker   Linebacker
                        LB            LB

      M    End    Tackle    Nose  Guard      Tackle    End
L     E    DE      DT           NG            DT       DE
I     N
N
E          OE     OT    G     C     G    OT      OE
           End  Tackle Guard Center Guard Tackle  End

O
F                               QB
F     B                    Quarterback
E     A                                       WB
N     C                                    Wingback
S     K          HB
S     S       Halfback
I                               FB
V                             Fullback
E
```

passed over. This goes for the allocation of playing time also. A negative attitude is costly.

I believe football is generally good for a kid with a bad attitude. Most sports quickly teach kids the price they pay for acting up, so they have a chance to deal with it. They want to play so they try to change. Hopefully, they get a coach who helps them control their emotions, instead of one who makes it worse; I've seen coaches get pretty nasty with a kid who needs a friend, and even drive the kid away from the game.

At some point, a player may get upset because his visions of scoring touchdowns have been dashed by an assignment to another position. I touched on this earlier but it bears repeating. He'll get over it! Don't exacerbate his frustration. He will learn how to have just as much fun tackling ballcarriers or opening holes for them. Remind him that a coach has to go with the faster guy in the back-field, that it's a team sport, and that he should just try to be as good as he can be at the assigned position.

There is a position on the field for each child. Coaches vary as to their views. Let's talk a bit more about each specific position. Please keep in mind that the general basic skills were covered in detail in chapter three and won't be discussed here in any depth. The idea here is to focus more on the nature of each position, and what the player needs to understand.

OFFENSIVE POSITIONS
Center
The center is just that—he plays the center of the line. His role is to snap the ball to the quarterback, avoid a fumble, and still make a good block on his man. He has to have perfect timing synchronized to the quarterback's cadence, or his hike will be late and his team will be offside.

The center has a slightly different stance from the rest of the line. His feet are spread wide and his hips must be high to allow for easy passage of the ball between his legs. The legs are positioned fairly evenly so as not to trip the quarterback. The weight is moderately forward on the ball. Kids often need two hands on the snap, although one hand is better, freeing up the other to deal with the opponent. The center's head may be in, but not beyond, the neutral zone between the front and rear of the ball. The head is up and is over, but not past, the end of the ball. The arm is extended and he turns and tilts the ball as is needed for a good snap. (See Figure 25.)

The center must snap quickly at the precise time. A very quick, firm snap is essential. The elbow bends slightly and he releases the ball to the quarterback. Of course, a center practices the snap thousands of times. Usually the quarterback wants the ball on a certain angle to fit his hand, with the laces hitting his hand by the fingertips. Different quarterbacks do it differently—this is why fumbles occur often in a game when quarterbacks are switched. The correct angle of the snap must be worked out. The center's hand also needs to be well forward on the top of the ball so that it is opposite the quarterback's hands upon transfer.

The center may step forward as he snaps. It may be a simultaneous motion, stepping and snapping. This is true only for the center; other linemen can't begin to move forward until the ball is already in motion. The center's first step must be very quick and should be straight forward, not to the side, and he should step with the foot closest to the side where the play will go. He angles his head to the runner's side and gives a quick pop to the opponent. (See chapter three for snapping on punts and kicks.)

Guards

On each side of the center are the guards. Offensive linemen all need strong legs since their principal job is to drive opponents away from their positions. However, guards also need to be quick. The guard often pulls out along the line of scrimmage to trap an opponent charging across the line, hitting him from the side. Guards also lead the runner through a hole. We discussed pulling skills earlier; the basic idea is to take a short step and push off with the down hand and with the foot opposite the direction of the pull. Bending his knees, the guard stays close to scrimmage and jolts the opponent. (See Figure 26.)

Guards need to use their entire body more than other linemen—cross-body blocks, crab blocks (see chapter three on blocks), whatever they can do to interfere with their opponent. Guards often get to trap the noseguard. However, the toughest defender on the field is usually the linebacker, and guards most often draw him. They must use their quickness against an equally quick opponent, and somehow stay between him and the ballcarrier. Blocking linebackers is clearly the toughest job for the offensive guard.

Tackles

Next to the guards are the tackles. I played this position on offense for a few years. Tackles are usually the biggest linemen. They generally block straight forward into a defensive tackle who is just as big as they are. Sometimes they block a linebacker or an end, or they go downfield to block a defensive back if the play goes to the opposite side of the field. They rarely pull, although it does occur occasionally. Size and strength are needed since this position in-

FIGURE 25
THE CENTER

Center is a tough job, and it takes a special kid to play center. The form here is excellent. Note that the other offensive linemen are lined up too far back.

FIGURE 26
The tackles and guards must move the defense away from the ball.

volves pretty much a one-on-one, straight ahead, short distance power struggle between two big players.

Offensive running plays, as will be discussed later, usually are dives up the middle, slants off-tackle (outside the tackle between him and the end), or wide sweeps around the end. On dives up the middle, the tackle shoots forward a step and stays between his opponent and the ball. However, on wide plays the defender has the outside advantage and so the job is much tougher. On sweeps, the idea is to delay the opponent from penetrating. Off-tackle plays, however, require the best effort. The opponent must be driven out of the area and turned away. This is the toughest job for the tackle, although a cross-block pattern helps.

Ends

The end needs to be tall and quick enough to catch short passes, but he must also be strong enough to block the defensive end and even the big defensive tackle when called to do so. In fact, the tight end spends most of his time blocking, and these skills must be worked on even more than receiving. Great tight ends are also great blockers. I played offensive end in my earliest years (before I got so big that I could block better than I could catch and was moved to tackle!). I truly loved this position since I got a chance to catch passes.

A very effective pass is a quick slant where the tight end dashes directly toward the middle, and the quarterback, who doesn't even drop back, fires the ball to him from close range. It's a tough pass to catch since it must be a hard-thrown one, but it's quite effective. Often a defender tries to jam the end—just give him a shot to slow him down—and of course this can eliminate the effectiveness of a quick slant pass.

A split end is an end who lines up at least several yards from the tackle and is primarily a pass catcher. The end's stance is similar to that of the other linemen. He is usually a yard or so outside the offensive tackle.

Often, the end is called upon to block downfield. These blocks are always difficult since defensive backs are very quick and agile and can use their hands fully. Usually the best that can be hoped for is just to slow them down a step, but that is also important. Kids often don't regard downfield blocking as important, yet a good downfield block, more than any other block, can spring a touchdown. Remind your son that he must play until the whistle blows, and to keep blocking someone.

Wide Receiver

Split ends, wide receivers and running backs all go out for the long passes. They line up very wide to try to ensure only one-on-one coverage. They need great speed, the quickness to fake a defender (see chapter three on receiving), and the courage to concentrate on receiving a pass while about to be hit hard. At the pre-high-school level, football is not a passing game since there are usually as many interceptions as completions. However, the wide receiver is still out there, waiting for his day to see the long pass sailing toward him against the blue sky. This is one of the truly great moments in all of football. Fans hold their breath. Things seem momentarily suspended; the ball is high in the air. No downfield contact is allowed while the ball is in flight, and the fleet-footed players are running at full throttle to snatch the ball from the air. Long pass receptions are clearly the most popular plays in the Pros, and they are the most beautiful to behold.

Halfbacks

Halfbacks are usually the fastest kids on the offense and they do most of the ball carrying for that reason. They spend some time blocking for the other backs and can also go out for a pass, but their primary job is to advance the ball. They run off-tackle or wide, usually leaving the short yardage, straight forward dives for the bigger fullback. I covered the stance, the pivot, and running skills in chapter three. The quick snap of head and shoulder, the pivot into the direction of the play, and then the step-out are the keys to a good, quick start. It also is essential not to tip off the defenders by looking or leaning in the desired direction before the hike. Remember, the linebackers are carefully scanning the halfbacks' faces and stance for any clue as to the play.

Halfbacks must move with explosive quickness in an endeavor to outrun the field, especially on wide sweeps or end runs. The moment of decision occurs when a defender approaches. Cut back? Try to dance and spin around? Lower the shoulder and ram forward, happy to settle for a few extra yards? The cut back and the fancy steps could spring long yardage, but also can lose a yard. The running-hard approach is more conservative and usually gains a few yards. The halfback needs to learn what he is most successful at doing. Remember, a few yards are a very valuable piece of territory! They can be the difference between a first down and losing possession. I generally like to see kids run hard and get the few extra yards, but the real key is for a player to follow his instincts.

Fullbacks

As noted earlier, fullbacks are usually the biggest and strongest of the running backs. They are asked to run the ball up the middle, usually on a straight dive play to one side of the center. They are expected to pick up a couple of yards regularly in short yardage situations. They run low and hard, with their heads up. They are expected to hit the hole very hard. It may not be a big hole, and they must capitalize on any advantage their blockers give them. Fullbacks don't dance much; they run hard and low and need a lot of momentum. They rely on their momentum to push the tackler back so the fullback can fall forward, gaining every extra inch possible. Short, quick steps and churning legs can propel a fullback as he falls for an extra yard or so. Usually both hands are pressed over the ball, holding it firmly to the stomach.

Fullbacks do a lot of blocking. They lead the halfbacks on sweeps, off-tackle runs or even dives. They block for the quarterback on passing plays. They must take fake handoffs and convincingly draw linebackers to them as they pretend they have the ball.

Quarterbacks

This quarterback is a top athlete, able to handle the ball securely, agile in traffic, and able to pass accurately even if on the run. He has good vision and a strong arm. He must know what everyone does on every play, and therefore needs to be quite intelligent. The quarterback must be a natural leader, able to motivate the players and to control his own intensity. He must take charge on the field and gain the respect of his teammates. His footwork must be precise. Fakes must be very convincing; good habits are necessary here. The handoff must be secure and, of course, passes must be accurate. The quarterback must learn when to throw, when and how to throw the ball away, and when to take a sack. He needs to understand when to scramble to avoid a loss of yardage. When a play breaks up, or someone misses an assignment, the quarterback must be able to react, improvise, and go with the flow of the play. Chapter three already covered the fundamental basics of passing and handoffs.

The worst thing for a quarterback is to fumble constantly, and it happens frequently at the youth level. Fumbles are killers to an offense trying to move the ball downfield and are most painful to coaches when they result not from contact but from bad ball handling. Repeated practice taking snaps is mandatory. A quarterback must take the snap securely *before* he pulls back. Premature pulling back from snaps, perhaps from a slightly late snap, causes many fumbles. There is no better way to take the steam out of a drive than to drop the snap. To prevent a dropped snap, the quarterback must get low, bend the knees, and get the hands under the center's crotch far enough to secure the snap. Sharp, quick moves are necessary so the backs can run the ball through the hole before it closes. I often hear parents screaming for blocking when in fact the hole was there but delay in the backfield was the real problem.

The quarterback lives in the eye of a swirling, grunting, clawing hurricane. He must stay poised. He can't worry about whether someone else is doing his job, but must go about his job with calmness and precision. Jerky, panicky moves lead to fumbles or cause a quarterback to trip or collide with his own players. He must also keep the offense coordinated and stay within the twenty-five seconds allotted to get a new play going after each down. He must know his personnel and try to find out where the defense is mismatched and where it is weak. When all else fails, he should rely on his most consistent teammate.

DEFENSIVE POSITIONS
Noseguard

This position, head-on to the offensive center, takes a special kind of kid. Action comes from all sides, very quickly. The most valuable piece of turf in the game is usually the one the noseguard stands upon. The offense often double-teams or traps him to get that piece of ground. So the main objective of the noseguard is to hold his ground.

His stance is a bit more solid and balanced than that of his teammates on the line. (See Figure 27.) Often the noseguard's stance is a four-point stance to ensure a low, well-braced charge. The worst thing for a noseguard to do is to stand up too quickly because, especially if he is double-teamed, he will be easy to move away. His charge should include a good shoulder jolt. Then he must crawl and scrape his way forward, always low enough that he cannot be driven away. The noseguard can submarine (dive low into the gap) and scramble back to his feet. Another good move is to dive over a low-charging center. But, most often, the noseguard jolts, sheds and scraps like all linemen, just a bit lower. Even if he is on hands

FIGURE 27
THE NOSE GUARD

The toughest position in football is the nose guard. He lines up head to head with the center. The nose guard here is in excellent form, low, poised, even with the nose of the ball.

and knees he is at least blocking the hole, slowing down the runner, and piling up bodies in the middle.

When double-teamed, the noseguard hits one blocker with his shoulder and fights off the other with his hands, turning his body sideways to claw his way through the seam between two blockers. Remember this is not a wrestling match; the idea is to shed. A major fault with defensive linemen (tackles and ends) is that they tend to focus too much on wrestling with their opponents. As stated in chapter three, the idea is to hit the defender to neutralize his charge and to shed him quickly. The noseguard must get rid of the blocker as fast as possible, not play with him! It's not a contest to see who is stronger, but a contest to get away from the blocker.

Defensive Tackle

The foundation of the defense is at the tackle position. The noseguard is expected to ward off the runners and to stack up the middle ground; however, the tackle is expected to earn his name by tackling, tackling, tackling. Defensive tackles are usually the biggest and strongest kids on the team and are also aggressive enough to hold ground, penetrate, and bring the ballcarrier down. As with the noseguard, the tackle must hold his position. Tackles are responsible for tackling the ballcarrier on off-tackle plays. The main area they are responsible for is head on. The noseguard is often double-teamed, so the dive play up the middle must be looked for, although this play is the linebacker's main responsibility. At the least, tacklers must hold their ground, and they should penetrate if possible. On short yardage they hold and protect inside; on long yardage they penetrate, looking for a pass rush and a possible sack. They are always under control, prepared for the possible trap.

Tackles usually line up on the outside shoulder of the offensive tackle on a five-man line. The inside foot is back and it steps first, while the front foot drives inside toward the pressure. Remember, as noted above, defenders don't wrestle! Defensive tackles shed the blocker and drive a shoulder into the ballcarrier. They should avoid arm tackles since they are weak. However, if off-balance, tackles should grab whatever is available.

Most kids don't fully understand the effect a good hard jolt has on their opponent. They use more of a shiver, hitting the blocker with their outstretched hands. Sometimes it looks just like they are playing patty-cake! A shiver move works for the end and the linebackers, but a down lineman is much better off dealing out a good shot and *then* using the forearm and hands to shed and hunt for the ball. Keep saying, "Hit, shed and hunt."

Defensive End

Defensive end is a great position. I loved it when I played it. These kids are usually tall with good upper body strength to hold off blockers. Usually a defensive end has to ward off multiple blockers before he gets to the running back on an end run.

The defensive end is responsible for the outside, that is, for the wide running plays. He should penetrate for several steps, then turn and force the play to the inside where there is always more help and less running room. A defensive end is often blocked by a pulling guard, or by a fullback on an off-tackle play, and his job is to keep those plays to the inside and to force the action even farther inside. On a pass play the end is a key pass rusher, and, like the legendary Lawrence Taylor, formerly of the New York Giants, he has a great angle to crash in on the quarterback.

The end stands up, arms at the side, crouched down a bit. He positions himself a bit outside the offensive end, or a yard or so off-tackle if the offensive end is split. (See Figure 28.) The inside foot is back, and this foot steps forward first. He quickly penetrates a bit and then turns to face the play. The end should penetrate several yards, to guard against the sweep, but also look to crash in on the off-tackle play or pursue a run to the other side. He must not be too quick to pursue, but look first for a possible reverse play before he leaves the area. The shiver charge described in chapter three is usually the most effective weapon for the defensive end to use to ward off blockers.

The end, as is the case with all linemen, must be under control. He should not leave his feet if at all possible—particularly during a pass rush—since a faked pass can take him out of the action and

FIGURE 28

The defensive end, #79, is in good position—slight crouch, hands out, inside foot back.

thus open up the outside area to a scrambling quarterback. The biggest mistake that ends make is getting faked inside, believing that it's an inside run. I remember it happening to me, and I remember the terrible feeling as I watched the real ballcarrier sweep untouched around my end on his way to big yardage. The end must hold the outside under all circumstances.

Linebacker

Linebackers are usually the toughest kids on the field. They are the heart of the defense. Their job is to figure out where the ball is going and to stop it. While a defensive lineman is expected to get blocked, perhaps double-teamed, and does not have the element of surprise, a linebacker has fewer excuses. He stands freely, with a few yards of space to react to the action. He must have a lot of upper body strength to throw off blockers, the agility to avoid them if possible and a pounding aggressiveness.

Linebackers line up in a standing stance, crouched and balanced,

FIGURE 29

LINEBACKERS

The three linebackers are the key to the defense. They are the second line of defense, just behind the linemen, and quickly penetrate holes from their standing position.

while leaning forward on the front of the feet, hands down and palms out, a yard or so behind the line of scrimmage. (See Figure 29.) He should scan the offense for clues as to where the play will go. Usually the offensive guards are the best clues, since on the snap they often move in the same direction as the ball. (I will review the keys to reading offensive motion in chapter five.) The linebacker must meet an approaching blocker with great strength and vigor, drive his forearm or straight arm into the blocker's upper body to neutralize him, and then quickly shed him. He must directly address the head-on blocker, give a blow, shed, sidestep, and hunt the ballcarrier. The inside linebacker usually goes directly to the hole.

During a pass play, the outside linebacker angles and looks to the flat on his side to pick up any receiver heading there and then prepares to cover that receiver. While outside linebackers have responsibility for the flat, inside linebackers mainly are concerned with defending against the short pass over the middle or a quarterback scramble.

Defensive Backs

The deep backs, safeties and cornerbacks are fast, tough kids and are the last line of defense. They must come up and tackle anyone who gets past the defensive linemen and linebackers. Most important, they must catch the breakaway runner and prevent a score. They must be in great shape and have good endurance, because in this position they run a lot. They head into downfield pursuit whenever the ball goes to the opposite side. The biggest mistake a defensive back can make is to fail to get into pursuit to cut off a breakaway runner. The concept for the secondary is always to rotate into pursuit; that is, they first back up and then circle toward the other side of the field.

Backs must make aggressive tackles but always be under control. They are often the last defender, so a missed tackle costs the team a high price. They generally want to edge to the outside of the runner, if possible, and force him inside, where there may be some more defensive help.

In a passing situation, the deep backs *always* look to intercept. They must expect to intercept, anticipate it, and try to catch the ball. The second biggest mistake they can make, however, is to let a receiver get behind them. They should never let the receiver get too close to them, so they always have some room to react to a change of speed or direction.

Now that you've learned about each position, I'll introduce some formations and patterns.

Chapter Five

CONCEPTS, FORMATIONS, PATTERNS

Here it starts to get a bit more complicated. I earlier discussed one difference between football and other sports in that it involves more desire and strength than skill. (Please understand, I do not mean this disparagingly; desire is just of greater importance. Skills are still quite important.) Another major difference is that the action on the field is much more controlled compared to other sports. Each offensive play is fully and precisely diagrammed and repeatedly practiced. Boys line up on the practice field and run through play patterns endlessly. They are expected to run plays smoothly. Blocking assignments are carefully planned out and passing routes are measured to the step.

Other sports have play patterns, but not as precisely worked out as in football. Basketball has specific offensive patterns, but there is much more flexibility. Soccer is at the other extreme and flows more according to general motion concepts. In football, play is largely preprogrammed, although players also need to be able to react to the situation at hand to some extent, as in all sports.

It is not the purpose of this book to get too deeply into the most complex aspects of the game. This chapter will discuss some general offensive and defensive *concepts*. It will also describe some specific formations and play patterns used in youth football. You can help a player greatly if you discuss the underlying concepts of offensive and defensive play with him. This will help him to open and broaden his perception of what's going on around him. Once a player understands why things are done a certain way, he can perform more intelligently.

OFFENSIVE CONCEPTS
Control Possession of the Ball

The bread and butter play of football is the *power running play*—
the dive up the middle or the slant off-tackle. If a team can successfully and consistently run the ball and slowly chew up yardage,
gaining 4 or 5 yards per play, then they will use up a lot of time.
This means that the other team will have the ball themselves for
less time. At youth levels, a good drive down the field, let's say 70
yards, takes about fifteen plays and can consume an entire quarter
of play. The other team can't score if they don't have the ball! Luck
is a large part of football, as in any sport, and teams do often get
lucky and break a big play for a score. But if you reduce the amount
of time that the other team possesses the ball, you reduce the odds
of their making such a play.

Football is much more of a running game at the Pop Warner level
than it is in high school. However, as mentioned earlier, the big
running plays are often wide sweeps by a really fast kid who outruns everyone and breaks away for a score. Yet the more conservative run up the middle is the cornerstone of good offense.

On first down the idea is to run a slant between the tackle and
the end and get 5 yards. Then you have two more shots at the next
5 yards. If your team can do this regularly, they will be successful.

Open a Hole; Penetrate the Defensive Line

If you want to advance the football, you need to open a hole in the
defensive wall so the runner can get by. Therefore, the primary
objective of every running play is to get the ballcarrier through the
first line of defense. If you do that, you will make at least 4 to 5
yards, and perhaps the runner will have time to put a move on the
defensive secondary and get more yardage.

Sure, a really strong kid can block a defensive lineman who is
ahead of him and just shove him out of the way, creating a hole.
However, younger kids are usually of similar strength, so you have
to get smart. The key to opening a hole consistently is usually in
slant blocking, that is, blocking from an angle.

If you can get your blockers into position where they are attacking their target defender from an angle, their job will be much easier. It's tough to block big, strong defensive tackles head on. They are usually the strongest players in the game. So, if you can approach them from the side, you avoid their strength. Plays are usually designed to provide as much slant blocking as possible.

Lead the Play Through the Hole

Often you get a hole opened up on the line, but a linebacker or defensive secondary player eludes a blocker and heads to the hole. It is very tough to make that initial block on the linebacker, so they often get to the hole when they see it forming. The offensive response is to have someone lead the play through the hole. You send a blocker into the hole ahead of the ballcarrier to block out the first defender who gets to the hole. You usually send a blocking back or pull a guard to do this job.

If all of these efforts fail and the hole is not opened, or perhaps it closes very quickly, then the runner is on his own. He can try to bull his way through for a yard or two, or change direction and try his luck elsewhere, looking for daylight.

When to Run or Pass

If it is third down and 2 yards to go for a first down, the odds are that you can pick up the 2 yards with a power play diving up the middle with your strongest running back, usually the fullback. However, if it's third down and 9, or, you got a penalty and it's second down and 19, then you have a long way to go. Since running plays usually average only several yards each, the odds are better to throw the ball in long yardage situations. A pass play can get 10 to 15 yards—much more if the receiver can make a move and avoid the first tackler.

Screen or Draw a Rushing Defense

I noted earlier that a defender's primary job is usually to control his area. There is a passive aspect that just says, "Don't let anybody get by." However, sometimes the defense gets ahead of themselves and finds that they can easily penetrate the offensive line to get into

FIGURE 30
TRAP BLOCK ON A DRAW PLAY

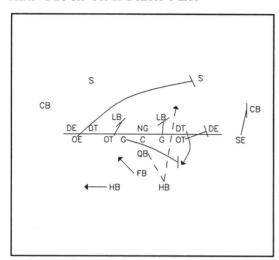

The defensive tackle comes across toward the right halfback and is trapped by the left guard.

the offensive backfield. This is disaster for the offense. A good coach will spot this and use the defensive momentum to help his team.

In such a circumstance, a screen play should be tried. The blockers give the rushing defenders a jolt to slow them up and then let them go. The quarterback drops back and then lofts a soft, short pass over the onrushing defense to a receiver who now has the blockers in front of him.

Trap blocks are also useful against onrushing defenders in a *draw play.* Here, the running back hesitates a second to give a pulling lineman time to get to his blocker. Then the quarterback hands off the ball and, just as the tackler thinks he will make a big tackle in the backfield, he is creamed from the side and taken out of the play. (See Figure 30.)

Misdirection
Another useful play concept is to sweep the backs in one direction to get the defense moving that way, then hand off to one back who counters against the flow. The blockers then have it easier since the motion pulls the defense to lean away from the actual play. However, if the defense is keying on the linemen and not the backs, this does not work as well.

Sweep Your Speedster

A coach must go with the hand he is dealt. If he has an extremely fast running back, then he can run him wide around the whole pack. Again, the main idea is to get past the defensive line and get that all-so-valuable 4 to 5 yards per carry. So, one way to get past the line is simply to run around it. A *pitchout* is a play designed to do just that.

In a pitchout the speedster lines up off-tackle and darts outside immediately upon the snap. The quarterback quickly laterals or pitches the ball underhand to the speedster, who then sprints to the sideline and tries to turn the corner and get some yardage. On such a play he is on his own. No blockers can get out fast enough to help much. It's just speed against speed. If a coach is blessed enough to have someone with such speed, the sweep play becomes a great tool.

Spread Out the Defense

When a team runs up the middle a lot, the defense tends to bunch up in the middle. The offensive coach can force the defense to open up a bit by putting a few wide receivers split out along the line of scrimmage or running a sweep or some pass plays to spread out the linebackers and secondary.

Take It to the Airways

As mentioned earlier, few passes are thrown at the youth level. The kids don't catch as well, the passes are not accurate, and pass blocking is usually poor (for reasons I can't understand, since pass blocking is the easiest thing in football). A passing game is usually dangerous, with a high potential for interceptions. The toughest part about youth passing seems to be the timing. Quarterbacks tend to hold the ball too long. They don't hit the receiver when he is in the seam, that is, in an open area between defenders. I have often seen a kid wide open across the middle, but the quarterback didn't pass the ball until the receiver reached the deep coverage and was no longer free. In any event, if a team is up against a tough defense and cannot run the ball, they have to go to the air and hope to get

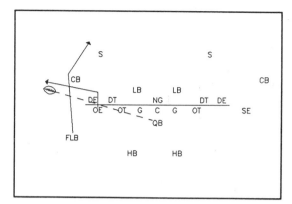

FIGURE 31

PASS TO THE FLAT

The wide receiver, here a flanker back, takes the cornerback deep, and so the tight end should be free in the flat.

FIGURE 32

QUICK SLANT PASS

The tight end slants directly across the middle with a very quick dash and grabs a pass. The quarterback doesn't even drop back, but just throws quickly.

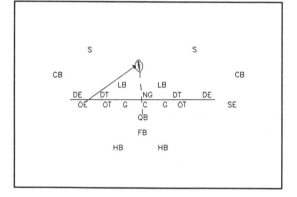

lucky. Believe it or not, it can happen sometimes.

I believe the most effective passes at the youth level are passes to the tight end in the flat, crossing behind a wide receiver who slants in. (See Figure 31.) For some reason this area is often open. The deep bomb is a dangerous play, and passes across the middle usually find a lot of congestion. But a *screen*—a short pass to the flat—is a good tool, particularly if the quarterback has speed and can roll out toward the sidelines. If the pass is across the middle, I recommend very quick, short passes. The quarterback doesn't even drop back but tosses it over the middle to a big tight end who finds some open space. It must be very quick. The backs head to each side of the center to stop a blitz and/or freeze the linebacker. (See Figure 32.)

Razzle-Dazzle

It's a fancy term—an over-glorified collection of trick plays that usually means a team can't overpower the defense and has to resort to complicated plays like reverses or flea-flickers. A *reverse* is a play in which the quarterback hands off to one running back going wide, who in turn hands off to another player going the opposite way. The idea is to get the defense going one way and then to have a speedster suddenly switch the other way around the whole pack. A flea-flicker is a play in which the quarterback hands off to a running back who takes a few steps forward and then turns and flicks the ball back to the quarterback, who then throws a long pass. The idea is to get the defensive backs to think it's a running play and thus come forward, while a receiver scampers past them for the long pass. There are also option plays (see glossary).

Razzle-dazzle can break open a big play, but it can also lead to a big loss when the defense is not outsmarted. The plays take a long time to execute, and a lot can go wrong. You don't see too much of this action in youth football.

DEFENSIVE CONCEPTS

A special feeling, a strong pride, comes from being a defensive ballplayer. Sure, the offensive backs get more glory, but even that is changing a bit as great linebackers such as Lawrence Taylor, achieve great recognition. I have pointed out repeatedly that the essence of football is the desire to overcome an opponent. Defense is made for this! Players have fuller use of the hands, whereas offensive players are significantly more constrained. Defense is mainly blood and guts, let me at 'em, clawing, scraping, head knocking, gritty, thumping football! However, some general concepts find their way through all the sound and fury, and they are most helpful to understand. Talk them over with your players.

Look for the Keys

Defenders must always be sensitive to tips or hints on where the play will go, as I discussed earlier. However, the best defensive tool, particularly at the less-complicated youth level, is to play according to the motion or flow of the offense, focusing particularly on certain players such as the offensive guard. Here are a few very specific keys to look for:

1. If the guard does not charge forward but steps back a bit in a stationary position, he is pass-blocking, and it's a pass play.
2. If he crosses the line of scrimmage, it's a running play, probably up the middle.
3. If he pulls in either direction, it's a running play in that direction.

The defensive backs can generally rely on these keys to help them react quickly and know what type of play is occurring.

Go With the Flow

The flow of a play is instantly revealed. The whole team suddenly shifts one way or the other, and the defense must respond immediately. The offense's first two steps are the most critical. The defense should try to get out in front of the flow, thus reducing the offense's advantage of surprise that comes with their knowledge of the timing of the snap.

Pressure the Middle

An offensive team that can drive up the middle for 4 or 5 yards a play dominates the game and keeps the other team's offense off the field. It follows then that the primary job of the defense is to shut down the power running game. Youth teams put their strongest players up the middle on defense. Once the defense bangs back a few offensive dive play attempts, the offense will be forced to go to lower percentage plays like sweeps or passes. It's much easier to stop a sweep or pass since they are more complicated plays to execute, and therefore the defense has time to get more people on the job. The offense has to rely much more on skillful execution to pull off wide plays. However, up the middle is power territory. The team that controls the middle of the line has a decided advantage.

Contain and Force the Play Inside

In soccer, the ball is forced outside, wide away from the goal. In football, however, the objective is to keep the runner inside where there is always more defensive help. The primary job of the defensive end—or outside linebacker, depending on the formation—is to turn the wide running play inside. Cornerbacks likewise are told to approach the man from the outside and turn him in where teammates are hopefully in pursuit. Most of the big gains on running plays come when a back somehow gets by the outside man and then sprints down the sideline.

Pursuit

How often during a youth game do you see defensive personnel standing and watching a play that goes to the opposite side? It causes me to wonder whether coaches at youth levels teach this concept enough. I know when I played that the instinct to take a little rest when the action went the other way was quite strong. However, many times the action turns back, and thus pursuing the ballcarrier can lead to a big tackle and save a touchdown. Furthermore, the play could turn the far corner, and often a pursuing defender can take an angle that meets the runner downfield.

Of course a defender cannot get into pursuit if he is entangled with his blocker. This is why it is so important to keep the blocker away from the body, using the hands to push or shiver him away, shed him, and then engage in pursuit of the ballcarrier. Kids must be told to keep moving until the whistle blows. If the play goes the other way they must chase it, laterally at first to ensure against a reverse. Then they must head downfield at an angle that seems reasonable and run until they hear a whistle. Good pursuit wins close games.

Stunts

Defensive linemen and linebackers have a certain zone to defend. However, sometimes their primary positions are changed to confuse offensive blocking assignments. A *stunt* is a defensive play in which responsibilities are swapped. A defensive tackle, usually responsible for the outside shoulder area of his opponent, slants diagonally inside while the inside linebacker loops around him to cover the off-tackle play. (See Figure 33.)

FIGURE 33

STUNTS

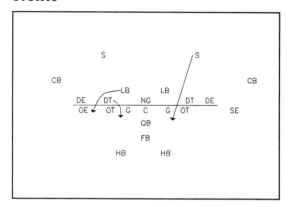

Two stunts are performed here. On the left, a tackle and linebacker exchange positions, the tackle slanting in and the linebacker looping around. On the right, a safety blitz occurs through the inside tackle hole.

Stunts can confuse offensive blockers and often result in easy tackles. However, a slipup here can also play into the hands of the offense. That tackle could get blocked on a dive up the middle, and the linebacker will have taken himself out of the play.

Another stunt that is often very effective is the *blitz*. One or more of the defensive secondary leave their positions and crash forward into the line. Again, these plays are quite often successful, confusing blockers and resulting in quick tackles and a loss of yardage. However, a substantial number of times they backfire, and the ball gets to the area vacated by the blitzing player. Since he is not there, a big gain of yards or even a score is possible. Stunts can work both ways, but more often they work very well for the defense.

Pass Defense

Hold the receivers; rush the passer; get the ball—these are the three keys to pass defense. It's unfortunate that pass defense has such a low priority at the youth levels because there are far fewer passes. But against a passing team, and certainly in high school, pass defense fundamentals are essential to stopping the aerial game.

The first key is to delay the receivers at the line of scrimmage for a step or two. Any delay in running their patterns takes precious time from the quarterback and adds substantially to the pressure on him. Pressure on a quarterback produces more errant passes than anything else. The defensive end gives a shoulder or forearm to the offensive end to delay him. A cornerback shivers a wide receiver at the line of scrimmage for a second. A second is all that is needed. The defensive back can hit a receiver only in the first five yards and cannot touch him after that. It's also important not to hold the receiver, which is a serious penalty. However, it is helpful to delay him for a step or two even if only by getting in his way.

The second key is to pressure the passer. If he gets four or five seconds to throw the ball, he can pass at will. Time gives receivers a real advantage to change direction, make fakes and get free. When the defensive line sees a pass play developing (it becomes evident quickly that it is a pass play when the offensive linemen do not cross the line of scrimmage), they must engage in a furious and frantic penetration to the quarterback. Nothing is more unsettling to a quarterback than to be under pressure. Pressure is the best weapon against passing accuracy, and a quarterback sack gives a decided momentum to the defensive team. Kids should be instructed to yell out "Pass!" as soon as they see a pass play develop—this word should act as a lightning bolt to the defensive line to charge the passer. Just the sound of their frenzy is upsetting to the passer.

The third key is to get the ball. Once the ball is in the air, it is anybody's ball. As long as the defender is going for the ball, he has as much right to it as the intended receiver. Therefore, once the ball is airborne, the defense should go for it. A defender can forget the receiver if he has a chance to intercept the pass. Otherwise, the defender must time his approach to slam the receiver as soon as he catches the ball. Anticipation is the defenseman's best friend. He should lash at the ball to jar it free and, if a teammate makes the interception, should not hesitate to block for him immediately.

OFFENSIVE FORMATIONS

At college and pro levels, and even at high school levels, a smart coach uses different offensive formations in each game to exploit individual weaknesses in the opponent's defense or to maximize

FIGURE 34

EARLY FOOTBALL FORMATIONS

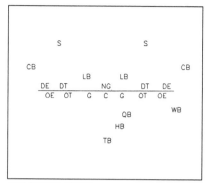

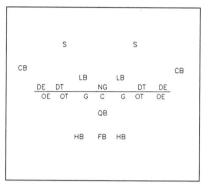

THE SINGLE-WING. In the single-wing the ball is hiked directly to a tailback or a halfback. The power is shifted entirely to one wing.

THE T. In the T formation all backs are able to hit any hole or block for any other back. A pure and powerful running formation.

the abilities of his own talent. The difference in various offensive formations pertains primarily to how the running backs and receivers are positioned. Some formations favor the running play and some favor the pass. The interior linemen nearly always line up the same way and vary only in how close they are to each other. However, the placement of the backs and receivers can vary greatly.

Figure 34 shows two formations, the single-wing and the T, that were very popular in the early days of football but are not used much anymore. Both of these formations are classic running or power formations and were used exclusively in the days before passing was allowed. In the deceptive T formation, the three running backs can strike anyplace on the line and can also block for each other. The ends stay in tight to block. The single-wing formation is even older than the T. It snaps the ball directly to a running back set 4 to 5 yards deep. The quarterback and a halfback line up to one side, with a wingback outside of the tight end.

The single-wing allows the offense to shift its strength to one side, adding greatly to the ability to run power plays to that side. Since this was before the rule requiring the offense to be set for a full second before the snap, the offense had a big advantage. However, the long snap created problems of its own, so the T was introduced to have the quarterback take snaps directly. It also increased the number of potential running backs to three, and this provided the running game with more blocking and more flexibility.

Then came the forward pass. It revolutionized the offensive formation. First came the *open formation*. It split one of the ends out wide along the line of scrimmage on one side and placed a flanker back out wide on the other side. The wide formation increases the chance for these receivers to face one-on-one coverage and spreads out the defense to the benefit of the running game. So the open formation posed a balanced threat for both the run and the pass. (See Figure 35.)

Other formations came along over the years. The *twin set formation* placed both wide receivers on the same side, allowing them to work crossing and other patterns off each other. The *veer formation* is also used sometimes. It's like a twin set formation except that the running backs line up wide, almost behind the tackles, to open things up more and make plays like the triple option possible.

Finally, the ultimate passing formation, the *single back* or *lone set back*, came on the scene, allowing for three wide receivers. Of course the lone running back has no other back to block for him, but some of the game's great running backs proved they could still get their yards, especially since the defense is so spread out to cover passes. The *shotgun formation* was popularized early on by the Dallas Cowboys. Here the quarterback takes the snap after lining up 5 yards behind center. Since it is quite awkward to hand off in this formation, it clearly signals a pass. It helps the quarterback since he can start looking at the defensive coverage immediately, without having to backpedal first. One or two backs are kept back to block in this formation.

In a player's early years of football, he will not see many purely passing formations. However, several good running formations are used. Modern coaches still like to use split ends to take a cornerback out of the action and open up the defense a bit. You see the *wishbone formation* a lot at young ages. It provides much of the running power of the old T formation, but the fullback plays forward a bit

FIGURE 35

COMBINED PASSING AND RUNNING FORMATIONS

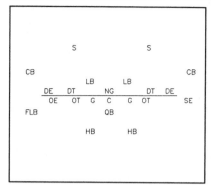

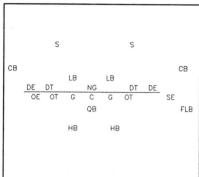

THE OPEN SET. In the open formation the defense is opened up for a balanced run or pass attack. Two backs are positioned to run or pass block and two receivers, a flanker, and a split end are wide for a pass.

THE TWIN SET. The twin set is just like the open formation except that both wide receivers are on one side. This allows them to make moves off each other such as crossing patterns.

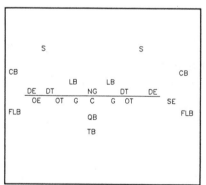

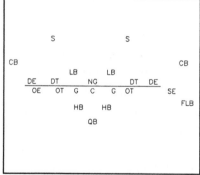

THE LONE SET BACK. This is one of the purest of passing formations and is used regularly in the Pro's. There is one single set back and three wide receivers. A variation could line up all three receivers on one side in an I formation, thus overloading the protection on that side.

THE SHOTGUN. The shotgun throws the ball back to the quarterback who can immediately focus on the pass pattern.

FIGURE 36

MODERN YOUTH LEVEL FORMATIONS

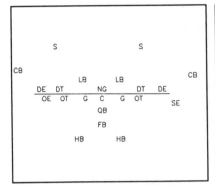

THE WISHBONE. This is a running formation much like the old T formation except that the fullback is pulled up closer to make the dive plays quicker and also block quicker.

THE I. The I formation is much like the open formation as it allows for a balanced passing and running game. The I shape lineup helps to conceal the play and gives more power up the middle.

to better enable him to block and also to hit the hole more quickly on straight dive plays. The *I formation* is another popular one. It is like the open formation except that the fullback and a tailback are in a straight line behind the quarterback. (See Figure 36.) Occasionally a team lines up in an unbalanced line that serves to confuse the defense. If the defense does not shift in this case, the offense has more players and thus more power to one side of the center.

Other formations are used and each coach has his own favorite. Hundreds, perhaps thousands, of offensive plays can be run from the various formations. The youth leagues are following the pro formations more and more. Each coach will have his own formations and it will be each player's job to memorize them. Parents can help by quizzing their child on his plays. Coaches get very irritated when kids forget plays, and I've seen it cost kids their starting positions.

Players need to know what every person should do *on every play*. At young ages kids are often shifted around to different positions. A coach makes changes all season. If he calls on a player to change positions, and the player has no clue how to play the new position,

FIGURE 37

LINE GAPS

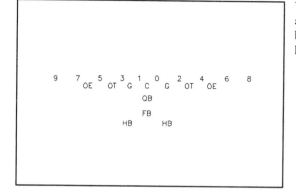

Your son's team may not assign numbers to gaps, but I always found it helpful to do so.

he will lose an important opportunity. So it pays to understand the concept behind each play and what everybody else has to do. At the very least, linemen should know what other linemen must do, backs other backs, and so on.

Players must approach each play from the standpoint of the area he is to block. The defensive formation on the play diagram, or the one he sees in practice, may change or the defense may be pulling a stunt. Usually at youth levels the defense comes with a five-man line. In this defense the noseguard lines up on the offensive center, defensive tackles on the outside shoulder of offensive tackles, ends outside the offensive end, and linebackers on the guards. However, sometimes a youth team uses a four-man defensive line or a six-man defensive line. A player must understand that his assignment is to block *whomever* is in his area of responsibility when he gets there, and to block them away from the path of the ballcarrier. Obviously, he must also know where the ballcarrier is going. A more general understanding of the play will help him become more valuable since he can react to changing circumstances in light of a full understanding of the concept of the play.

OFFENSIVE PLAY PATTERNS

The number of possible offensive plays is endless. They fall into general categories. The *gaps* between offensive linemen are often

FIGURE 38
OFFENSIVE PLAY PATTERNS

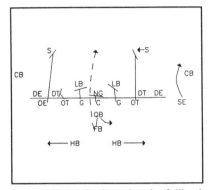

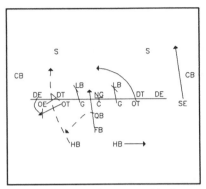

(a) In this simple dive play the fullback powers into the line.

(b) An off-tackle slant, cross block at the line, and fake to the fullback.

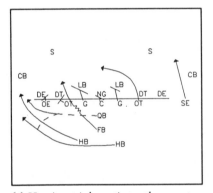

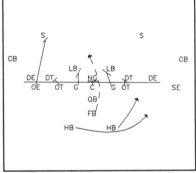

(c) Here's a triple option—the quarterback, looking at what the defensive tackle does, bellies the fullback and then can sweep out with the option of using either halfback.

(d) This is a counter-play to the fullback. The flow is to the right and he counters back to the left fullback.

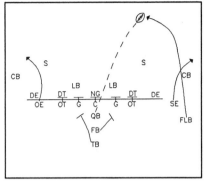

(e) Here's a deep post pattern (to the goal post); it's also known as a Hail Mary or deep bomb.

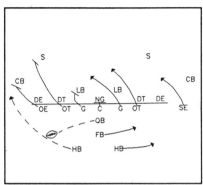

(f) The pitchout is another favorite—the halfback just outruns everybody.

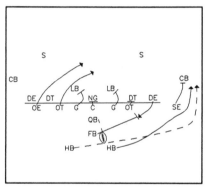

(g) On a typical sweep play, everybody heads east and tries to get the halfback around the sideline.

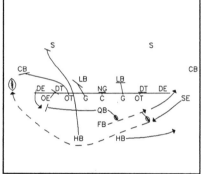

(h) A little razzle-dazzle reverse to a quick split end can catch a defense that goes into pursuit too quickly.

numbered. (See Figure 37.) Some plays are coded in a way that includes these numbers; for instance, 143 would signify that the #4 back (usually a halfback) will carry through the #3 hole between the left guard and tackle. The first digit signifies a straight running play, as opposed to a draw. Nowadays, however, plays usually just have names.

Some Concepts

A *dive* is a run up the middle to either side of center into the #0 or #1 hole. (See Figure 38.) A *slant* runs off-guard into the #2 or #3 hole. *Off-tackle* is another slant play into the #4 or #5 hole. An *end-around* goes to the #6 or #7 hole. The *sweep play* uses the #8 or #9 hole. Not all teams designate gaps with numbers. Some just use terms like dive, slant, belly, counter and sweep.

In *option plays* the quarterback runs wide with another running back on his outside shoulder. If a tackler approaches, the quarterback has the option of cutting inside or pitching the ball outside to the other runner. I've seen the *triple option play* in Pop Warner ball. Here the quarterback turns to hand the ball to the fullback. However, he rides the belly of the fullback and looks at the defensive tackle before releasing the ball. If the tackle commits himself forward, the quarterback releases the ball. If the tackle holds back, covering the zone, the quarterback takes the ball back and heads outside for a regular option pattern. More and more we see plays that give options depending on what the defense does after the play starts.

The series of diagrams in Figure 38 shows a number of play patterns that are useful from a wishbone offense, to give you a feel for what your son will be expected to learn.

DEFENSIVE FORMATIONS

As mentioned before, the idea on defense is to keep enough strength up the middle to force the offense to run wide or pass. Success up the middle is critical to winning football. Usually a middle or inside linebacker is the most critical to defensive success. I've also seen good noseguards terrify the offense, cause mis-snaps

FIGURE 39

DEFENSIVE FORMATIONS

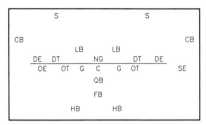

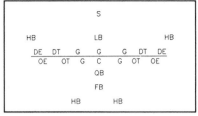

THE 54. The standard defense at the youth level and you will see a lot of it. It's been called the Oklahoma 54. It nicely balances against the run and the pass and equally distributes individual defensive responsibility across the line with defenders generally hitting gaps.

THE SEVEN DIAMOND. This is also called the seven gap since most linemen are in gaps. It's a short yardage defense with heavy responsibility on the half-backs.

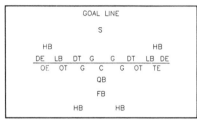

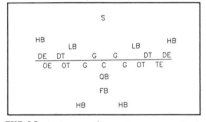

GOAL LINE. In this formation every gap is plugged, and the three defensive backs must assist by stopping the ball at the line.

THE 62. A six-man line, stronger against the run than the 54, especially off-tackle.

FOUR-MAN LINE. In this formation every gap is plugged, and the three defensive backs must assist by stopping the ball at the line.

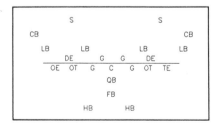

and fumbles, unnerve the quarterback, and generally wreak havoc in the offensive backfield.

Not as many defensive formations are employed as offensive, particularly at the young ages. The standard defense is a five-man line with two inside linebackers, two cornerbacks and two deep safeties. The four-man defensive line is used more in the Pros where there is more passing. (See Figure 39.) In short yardage situations a team goes to a six- or seven-man defensive line. The eight-man gap defense is used on goal line situations. I prefer the five-man line as a general defensive setup for kids. It seems to provide the flexibility and balance needed for youth play.

Chapter Six

THE PSYCHOLOGY OF COACHING FOOTBALL

ON WINNING

> Our society is ferociously competitive in spirit. Pressuring children too hard may turn them into adults so obsessed with being first that they get no joy out of life except in the narrow field of competition. They neither give nor get pleasure in their relationships with spouses, children, friends, and fellow workers.
> —*Dr. Benjamin Spock*

> Winning isn't everything; it's the only thing!
> —*Coach Vince Lombardi*

At the heart of how good a coach or parent you will be is how well you balance the need to win with your responsibility to develop healthy young people. This balance will affect your every action, your relationship with each player, the atmosphere on the field, and it will characterize the memory of your coaching experience for many years to come. Striking that balance involves a continuing struggle with the passions of competition.

The point is that *it is a balance.* Dr. Spock and Coach Lombardi both had a point of view grounded in experience. For instance, we all worry a bit about the total dedication required of young Olympic athletes, having sacrificed much of their youth for their quest. Yet, we know they have enjoyed moments of glory which seem to transcend life itself, achieving heights most of us only dream about.

It's not realistic, and therefore not helpful, to have people like

Alfie Kohn tell us in his book *No Contest: The Case Against Competition* (Houghton Mifflin) that analysis of years of prior psychological research proves that "competition is poison." That's like telling us not to breathe because the air is somewhat polluted! Nor do I think the proper balance was found by such as Eric Margenau, a renowned sports psychologist in his book *Sports Without Pressure* (Gardner Press, 1990) in which he suggested that "Competition is fine, but should be kept friendly with the emphasis on participation rather than outcome. Parents should not pressure a child to excel, *regardless of that child's abilities*." I disagree. Lets face it—we all know kids who could excel, but do not. They just need a little boot in the backside to get going.

By the same token, many of us will remember the ugly scene on national TV when competitive fires drove Ohio State coaching legend Woody Hayes to attack an opposing Clemson player on the field. And we cringed when young tennis star Mary Pierce, symbolic of many troubled young athletes, had to obtain a restraining order against her father from pressuring her. We're all too familiar with unbridled frenzy to win, often riding on the dark horse of fear of failure.

This issue goes to the essence of the human condition. It is part of our evolution. The answers are complex and most elusive. What is clear to me after many years of coaching and playing sports is that the answer is not to give up. I recently read in the *New York Times* that some schools are abandoning competitive interaction in their phys-ed programs to avoid damaging feelings of kids who are not outstanding. Isn't it better that kids learn about and prepare for success and failure in a controlled setting inside the relatively harmless gymnasium than in the crucible of adult life? We shouldn't abandon the struggle to succeed just because we haven't figured out how, as a society, to do it right. We couldn't quit if we wanted to. It's part of life, and we need to continue to work to find the best balance.

I think if we locked Coach Lombardi and Dr. Spock in the same room they would probably find common ground. Lombardi knew better than most coaches that the key to success in football was in knowing how to motivate athletes to win the personal struggle to do one's best, to improve beyond one's limits, spurred on by your team's goals. He said that the spirit, the will to win, the will to excel—these are the important things that transcend the game itself.

Joe Paterno, the legend-in-his-own-time coach of Penn State, talked about winning in his book *Football My Way* (Mervin D. Hyman, 1971):

> Nothing in life, including football, is worthwhile unless you enjoy it and gain something from the experience. Like a skier going down a mountain, you should be doing it for the sheer enjoyment of it, not because you have to win or are afraid to lose. Sure, we're trying to win football games and we're not going to be satisfied with anything less than a 10-0 record, but I don't want it to ruin our lives if we lose. I don't want Penn State to become the kind of place where a 8-2 season is a tragedy. You can't tell kids that a football loss is a tragedy because it's not. All I ask them to do is to give their best. If we win, Great! If we lose, it's not the end of the world. There is another game Saturday. I don't want my players crying. I want them to feel bad, but not ashamed. I'll never buy that stuff some coaches say that if a boy loses a game he is a loser for life. The coaches with that attitude, that winning is the only thing, don't belong in football.

Tom Landry, the great former Dallas Cowboys coach agreed in his autobiography, *Tom Landry* (Zondervan, 1990):

> If winning is the only thing that matters, then you'd do anything to win. You'd cheat. You'd sacrifice your marriage or your family to win. Relationships wouldn't matter. People wouldn't matter. Winning would be worth any price you had to pay. I don't believe that; after working with Vince Lombardi day after day for six years, I know he didn't believe it either. A more accurate reflec-

tion of his feelings would require a revision to that fa-
mous quote, to read "Winning isn't everything, it's the
effort to win that matters."

However, it's fair to say that Paterno and Landry do not represent
the majority view of NFL coaches, who must produce wins or lose
their jobs. This win-at-all-cost attitude filters down through college,
high school, and Pop Warner type leagues. I've seen it.

How you resolve the balance between winning and individual
development is up to you. If you recognize the need to strike a
balance, you are off to a good start. My own approach in coaching
is probably best characterized as a struggle back and forth around
that balance. When I find myself too focused on the win, I step
back a bit. Let's be honest—we don't see many "perfect models of
balance," since the emotions and competitive fires that naturally
arise on the football field during play can be quite powerful.

I believe most coaches want to build character and provide a
positive experience for each player while trying to win the game.
There are some who never really challenge their teams for fear of
upsetting the kids, and these "nice guys" don't do much damage.
Of course their players may never rise to the next level of play.
Other coaches, at the opposite extreme, feel compelled to win at
any cost, and the cost can be tragic for the fragile psyche of a young
boy. Find the middle ground.

Of course, the issues vary with the age of your team. At preteen
football levels, the emphasis is heavily on developing the individual. This is why most programs require that all kids play a certain
amount of time. By the time of high school varsity play, the balance
is more even. It should never get further than that, but the reality
of major collegiate play is that losing coaches don't last.

ON MOTIVATION

Rock, I know I'm going to die. I'm not afraid. But someday, Rock, when things on the field are going against us,
tell the boys, Rock, to go out there and win just one for

the Gipper. Now, I don't know where I'll be then, coach. But I'll know about it, and I'll be happy.
—*George Gipp*

Legendary Notre Dame coach Knute Rockne waited eight years until, during halftime in a big game against Army, he repeated these last words of his dying quarterback in what was to become the epitome of halftime motivation. It's a beautiful story, but coaches need to rely upon a lot more than halftime speeches to motivate their team. Sure, some coaches have that charismatic quality and can motivate a team just by the sheer strength of their personality. Rockne and Lombardi are the models of the "hero" coach. However, the rest of us more "mortal" guys need to consider motivational techniques that can help us get the job done. The secrets to good motivation are easily found in the growing science of *sports psychology*. Once considered mere gobbledygook, the mental aspect of competition is now a cornerstone of athletic development at the highest levels of amateur and professional sports. Many teams, including the U.S. Olympic program, have employed full-time sports psychologists.

It is not the purpose of this book to go in great depth into the psychology of sports. You will find aspects of psychology spread throughout this book, as well as in my books on coaching other youth sports such as baseball, basketball and soccer. I have used psychological insight throughout my twenty years of coaching, and you will probably agree that much of this is common sense, obvious to any caring adult. The first chapter of this book focuses directly on the right mental approach to the game. My *checklist* approach to teaching form is consistent with the mental checklist urged for athletes by sports psychologists. If you want to focus more deeply on this area, one of the best books I've read on this subject is *The Athlete's Guide to Sports Psychology: Mental Skills for Physical People* by Dorothy V. Harris, Ph.D., and Bette L. Harris, Ed.D. (Leisure Press, 1984). I will, however, discuss some emerging motivational techniques that seem to work best for youth football.

Attaboy!

There never will be a better tool than frequent positive reinforcement for young athletes. This is especially true for football. Since the coach so often has the occasion to bellow at players to get them psyched up, it becomes essential to liberally give out some *attaboys* for good effort. In *Kidsports: A Survival Guide for Parents* (Addison-Wesley, 1983), Dr. Nathan J. Smith, a consultant for the American Board of Pediatrics, studied two groups of coaches. He found that "the single most important difference in our research between coaches to whom young athletes respond most favorably and those to whom they respond least favorably was the frequency with which coaches reinforce and reward desirable behavior." A pat on the back, a smile, clapping, praise, a wink and a nod, as well as tangible rewards such as decals on the helmet or more playing time, all go a very long way toward motivating high performance. I would add to this concept that the rewards are even more effective when they emphasize outstanding effort as opposed to a great result. An athlete has complete control over the amount of effort he puts into his game. The result, however, is dependent on a number of things, many of which are beyond the individual's control. Even corrective action, pointing out mistakes, should be sandwiched somehow within some positive comments; e.g., "Good try, Jack, next time drive the shoulder into the midsection and wrap the arms—you can do it!"

Football coaches spend a lot of time hollering, trying to motivate players, and developing that all-important *desire to overcome the opponent.* It's a tough sport, and kids can't be holding back. However, there is a line that shouldn't be crossed—humiliating a player. The idea is to be firm, to let players know that they can do better if they reach deeper into their gut. I like to ask players if they gave it their best shot. "Was that your best effort?" or "Don't you have more 'pop' than that?" Let a player know what you think about his *effort*, not himself. Don't personalize it. A kid can relate to trying harder, but he can't relate positively to your telling him he stinks. Explain the problem with fundamentals or form so that he *understands the concept.* Take time until he gets the idea. Be clear in how you communicate to players.

Most important, reward good effort openly and liberally. Praise a good jolt. Recognize hustle. Yell out, "That's football!" It can get infectious, with all players trying to hear the sound of a good pop.

We Are Family!

I've read the autobiographies of many great coaches. The one constant in all of their stories is their ability to relate closely to the different individuals on their team, and create a family-type environment. Each kid is different, whether on a team or in a family, and each one needs a personal approach. Most important, even the lowest substitute should be treated with the same respect as the best players. I used to start each season with a team discussion on what it means to be on a team. I would tell the players that for the rest of the season they are all friends. They are all in a special relationship with each other. I tell them they should say hello in the school hallways, and help each other out both on and off the field. I never tolerated criticism of a teammate on the field, and would quickly bench any offender. Kids were expected to urge each other on, to quickly tell a teammate to put a mistake behind him. I promoted team dinners and outings and moved to break up cliques.

Joe Paterno said in *Football My Way*, "If we could get that feeling—-that 'we' and 'us' instead of 'I' and 'me'—so you can feel the love and respect for each other, they lose that individuality for the good of the team. When they lose themselves in something they think is a bit bigger than they are, they will be tough to beat."

Teambuilding is a proven ticket to success. The concept is widely used in all walks of life, and is a staple of Japanese and American business organization. But it doesn't just *happen* because a bunch of kids are on a team. It happens when coaches work at it. Put it in the practice plan, talk to your assistant coaches about it, and opportunities to promote *teamness* will present themselves in abundance.

Set Goals

It may seem trite, but it is essential to proper motivation to set realistic goals for both the team and the individual. With specific goals, a kid has something clear and achievable to set his sights on. He is not responsible for the whole team, or for winning or losing. He is not overwhelmed and defeated by unrealistic expectations.

I think it's a good idea to have each player set his own goals under guidance of the coach. I usually offer the players a number of categories in which a few goals should be set. One category is conditioning, and the goals may be to double the number of push-ups they can do, knock a number of seconds off a 440 sprint or a mile, and increase their chin-ups. A second goal relates to specific skills for their position. It may be to improve the form of the *set* position or of the initial thrust, or to improve receiving techniques. A third goal relates to game performance, e.g., number of tackles. I might also suggest to a boy that he increase his self-confidence, his self-control, his relationship with certain teammates, or his effort at practice. I'll have this written down by the player, and we'll occasionally review progress. Don't set too many, just focus on key areas.

Frankly, I don't think motivational techniques vary with the age of the players. Positive reinforcement, team dynamics and expectations are as important for kids as they are for pros.

ON PEAK PERFORMANCE

The bane of coaches is whatever it is that makes a kid play great one day and fall apart the next. A kid gets knocked on his back during the opening series, and he winds up getting pushed around all day. Another kid doesn't get blocked, makes a good tackle, and suddenly starts to terrorize the line of scrimmage. One day the halfback can't find the hole even if he could roll through it sideways, other days his cutbacks seem transcendent.

Modern science tells us that it's all "upstairs," at least much of it, in how athletes cope with the stress of the challenge before them. Mental control begins with understanding the commonly known "fight or flight" instinct, that is, the natural impulse that arises in cornered animals to respond to a threat by fighting it or fleeing from it. It is a genetic reaction, inherited in humans from our earliest ancient ancestors. This reaction under game conditions can create a panic that distracts concentration and can even cause muscles to spasm. However, when controlled properly, it can lead the athlete to a zone of peak performance.

In its February 14, 1994, issue, *U.S. News & World Report*, in an article entitled "The Inner Game of Winning," reported on the research of Stanford University neurobiologist Robert Sapolsky. He found that the properly controlled response to challenge releases a desirable increase in adrenalin and sugar producing the sense of "heightened awareness and flow" associated with being in a peak "zone." The negative counterpart of this reaction, which he calls the "fearful" response, produces a bodily cocktail laced with a substance called "cortisol" which can "not only impair performance, but can also lead over the long run to damage of the arteries and liver and lead to depression."

Another interesting study, reported in the August 3, 1992, edition of the same magazine, was entitled, "The Mental Edge: The brain is the key to peak performance in sports and in life." Brian Hatfield of the University of Maryland reported that at moments of peak performance, the brain's left side, the analytic side, erupts in a burst of relaxing alpha waves, indicative of a relaxed trance-like state. This allows the right side of the brain, which controls spatial relations and pattern recognition, to control the body.

OK. What does all of this have to do with kids playing football? Well, for one thing, it helps us learn how to minimize that inconsistency we complained about at the beginning of this section. The research tells us what steps can be taken to create the conditions optimal to peak performance.

Some of this we already do, and have done so for years. The time-honored best way to produce a controlled response to game day excitement is constant repetition during practice. Much of this book deals with the need to repeatedly go over play patterns, form and concepts. This is so the responses become automatic and can occur even if the player is under stress or overly excited.

The studies both also suggest that a ritual-like approach to game day is conducive to the relaxed state of mind needed. A regular pattern of eating, exercise, dressing, and pregame discussion is highly recommended. Try to avoid any surprises or deviations. The preset mental routine should apply right up to each snap of the ball during the game. Players should be encouraged to run through a checklist of form (e.g., head up, prepare to jolt, drive the forearm into the midsection). Tell them to mentally image the play, imagine themselves with great form jolting the opponent, or dashing through a hole, eluding the grasp of a tackler. They do this right up to the hike of the ball. This stuff works! It is well accepted at the highest levels of sport. Tell kids that they need to prepare the mind, as well as the body if they are to reach their best potential.

Sapolsky notes that premature arousal of adrenalin hours before the game can result in the level in the blood dropping after a few hours, even to a point below normal at game time. This will lead to sub-par performance and is another reason to have relaxed and stable pregame routines. Certainly, don't have the team screaming and hollering in the bus on the way to the game. Many coaches now employ Zen-type meditations in the training programs, providing athletes with methods to cause relaxed states of mind at will.

Sports psychologists have anticipated this research for years in their support for mental imaging of athletic routines. Olympic athletes have been imaging their steps mentally for years. What we have now are clear scientific bases for these approaches. These techniques are useful at all levels of play. They are perhaps most needed at the youngest levels where kids have less ability to control the anxieties of competition. Relaxed game day rituals, mental imaging, affirmations as to self-esteem, mental checklists (such as contained throughout this book, e.g. a defender must charge, neutralize, shed, focus, drive and wrap a ballcarrier), are techniques that can be repeatedly practiced.

Get an Edge

Many coaches have some concept that they repeatedly use to focus players on achieving peak performance. I always told my players to try to *get an edge* over their opponent. We talked about how similar competitors usually are physically, and so the winner would be the one who gets some kind of edge over the opponent. This concept helped me to get kids to accept, for instance, the idea of improving their mental approach—as one way to get an edge. I would tell kids to double the number of pushups they could do, since the other kids on other teams probably weren't doing it.

Don Shula is the winningest NFL coach of all time. He used the concept to its fullest and named his autobiography, *The Winning Edge* (Ed Dutton & Co., 1974), after it. He said in the book, "It is my firm belief that the concept of The Winning Edge and our ability to drive it home to the players helped produce the perfect season we experienced in 1972." Need I say more?

ON KIDS

In the final analysis, youth football is about boys becoming men. You need to know that most boys come out for the team for reasons very different from what you would hope for. Many of them believe that football players are the in-crowd; football players get the attention of the girls, and so the boys know that joining is the thing to do. Others are looking to build themselves up physically, get in shape, or find a way to release pent-up frustration. Some do it just because friends do it, and so they are seeking camaraderie. Others do it because Dad told them they had to.

Most Pop Warner level players won't eventually start varsity at the high school level, and only a few of them may play in college. You will probably never coach a future Pro Football player. It is doubtful that they will remember much about last season twenty years from now, certainly not the scores of various games. But I guarantee you one thing. They will remember *you* for the rest of their lives. The memory of my coaches is etched clearly on my mind. I remember them vividly, for good or for bad. You will not remember all of the kids you coached, particularly if you do it for a number of years, but every one of them will remember you. How do you want to be remembered?

The relationship between a coach and a player is a powerful one. You are a not only a father figure (99.9 percent of football coaches are men), but you are the ultimate authority for what is, in a kid's mind, the most important thing in all of life. Through his football experience, he is learning important things about himself, and he will always associate this experience with you. I always viewed coaching as an awesome responsibility. You may want to ignore the larger picture, but sticking your head in the sand does not change what is really going on. There are many tools you can use to help you make the experience a good one, whether you win or lose as a team, but in the final analysis it comes down to whether you can accept the larger role of being both a coach and a friend.

Vince Lombardi, who coached St. Cecilia's High School in New Jersey at one point, spoke of the role of a coach in an interview recorded in *The Vince Lombardi Scrapbook* (Grosset & Dunlap, 1976). He spoke about high school coaches and said:

> Well, he's probably the only man in the whole school who can do anything about discipline. And to do that, the first thing I would tell that coach is to be himself. The number one objective you must have is to sell yourself to them, honestly, from the heart. What you are teaching has to be *what you are.*

Joe Paterno added:

> First of all, a coach has to be a teacher . . . not just of skills but of character qualities and some values in life. . . . He has to be a leader . . . to make the players identify with him, and to develop morale . . . . He must be able to develop three things in an athlete: pride, poise, and self-confidence.

It's much more than just x's and o's!

ON PARENTS

Interfering parents have become a major problem for coaches in most sports. It seems less so in football than for some other sports, and that may be because parents are usually sitting farther away from the team. In baseball, they are right on top of the team, and so their complaining seems more visible. Nonetheless, it is a problem in all sports.

I have no problem with the parent who is just trying to communicate with the coach and find out whether there is some problem they need to be aware of. But often they are argumentative and downright insulting.

Of course, you don't need to take any abuse from a pain in the neck. But before you get too defensive, think about what's going on. Most parents feel helpless when they see their son going through a bad time. Maybe he is not playing much and is having self-doubts. He may be acting up at home or school because of it. Parents feel the pain along with their kids. It's tough finding out you're not good enough. So hear them out. Give them some ideas that help them understand what the problem is, and perhaps you can focus them on things they can do to help their son. If the problem is how they feel you are treating the boy, tell them that your are "on" the kid because you think he can do better and that you are trying to arouse his potential. Maybe you can get some insight into what is troubling a young man or what is holding him back.

Most of all, keep in mind that *he's their kid!* They may feel a bit threatened by your control over their child. As a parent, I have had a few uneasy feelings about coaches. It's quite natural. A little patience on your part can defuse some strong emotions. You can turn a potential feud into something that helps the boy, and ultimately the team. Try it.

Chapter Seven

RUNNING A PRACTICE: FIVE KEY OBJECTIVES

Perhaps the most common question I get from parents who begin to coach a team in any sport is, "How do I start?" or "How do I run a practice?" The job starts early! A few weeks before the first practice (preferably even earlier), you should get the word out to your team, and to the other parents, that things will go much better if the players show up in decent shape. Football relies on both leg *and* upper body strength, so both ends require some attention. I feel it's best, particularly at grade school levels, to suggest that players come to the first practice able to run a mile or two without looking like they are about to collapse. They should also be able to do 25 to 50 pushups. So, they should work at least every other day to reach this level. At the high school varsity level, most programs will offer some supervised summer weight training. Also, it's good to get a head start on learning plays, so get diagrams of the key plays out to the team early. Most important, tell parents about this book!

There are several key objectives that you need to consider for each week's practice plan. Their relative importance will vary a bit as you get further into the season, and they also vary depending upon what age group you work with, but these concepts are always important and should be part of your plan for each practice.

1. Get the players in shape.
2. Understand each player's potential.
3. Work on individual skills for each position.
4. Work on team execution of plays.
5. Motivate, communicate, lead.

Football practices typically last around two to two and one-half hours. The practice the day before a game is much shorter, maybe an hour or so. My recommendation is to go a bit longer early in the season, two and one-half hours, and shorter in midseason, an hour and a half to two hours.

All five objectives should be considered each time you prepare a practice plan (I'll get to what a practice plan looks like a bit later). In a two and one-half hour practice, I would devote one-half hour to stretching and conditioning, one hour to individual skills development, and one hour to team dynamics. Early in the season you need more time on conditioning, speed and agility drills, and later in the season you need to spend more time on teamwork.

Let's discuss each practice objective.

GET THE PLAYERS IN SHAPE
It is of little use to have players know their plays and develop good timing, only to run out of gas in the second half of a game. Frankly, it doesn't take much to get grade school or high school kids into shape, and there is just no excuse when they aren't. The worst mistake is to assume that the kids will get themselves into shape. I knew a coach with a potential championship team who refused to waste much time at practice on conditioning. His team never came close to success.

Here are a few dos and don'ts about getting players in shape.

Warming Up
Make sure players warm up before practice. A few laps around the field at a slow pace should cause a sweat and warm up the major leg muscles. Tell your players that muscles are like bubble gum—unless they stretch slowly they will tear.

Don't expect that players will warm up sufficiently on their own. Tell them to stretch it out on their own before practice, but then get the team together to do it some more. Players get hurt too easily when not loose, and so you need to get it done. Start the team off with what I call the quick *Cali Set*: 25 jumping jacks, 25 push-ups, 20 partial sit-ups (bend knees, get shoulder blades off the ground), 20 trunk turns, and 6 neck bridges (start off real slow here with light neck pressure. After a while, while on the back, bridge the body between helmet and heel.)

Next, move on to leg stretches in what I call the *Stretch Set*. (See Figure 40.) These stretches should be done smoothly without jerking or straining.

1. *Toe-hand*: lying on the back with arms outstretched, alternately touch each foot to the opposite hand (10 times)
2. *Hurdler*: sitting on the ground with one leg forward and one bent backward, touch the forward toe, then slowly lean back stretching the back leg (reverse legs and repeat three times)
3. *Supine hamstring*: lying on the back, pull one leg to an upright straight position (reverse and repeat three times)
4. *Standing quadricep*: standing on one foot, grasp the other foot behind the back and gently pull it to the buttocks (reverse and do three for each leg)
5. *Thigh stretch*: standing with legs outstretched, slowly lean to one side, bending that leg, stretching the under thigh of the other leg (three for each leg)

FIGURE 40
Sitting toe touch

6. *Achilles and calf stretch*: place one foot a step in front of the other, lean forward and bend the front leg, stretching the lower part of the back leg (reverse and do four for each leg). No jerking movements, no bobbing up and down!

The captain can lead the exercises, and you can let him start this part of the practice while you get organized, check to see who is there, talk to coaches or parents.

Monitor Your Players

Evaluate the heat at all times when doing conditioning, and make sure none of the players get heat exhaustion, especially early in the season when it's hot and they are out of shape. Do this for the whole practice on hot days. On such days I prefer multiple brief breaks to one ten-minute midpractice break.

Don't overwork players. Some coaches have their kids running all the time all season long. The players are young, but there are limits even for the young. By the same token, there can be periods when players are just standing around. I believe that push-ups are the best single exercise for building upper body strength in kids (along with the hated sit-ups). Hand out sets of twenty push-ups or sit-ups freely. Tell the kids when it's not punishment. Tell them you are trying to give them an edge that they will need when they come up against their opponents. If a kid does a hundred push-ups a day, he will become quite strong! Judge what a player can do, and slightly push his limit. Don't ask him to do something that will embarrass him, though.

Improvement Drills

Avoid weight training for grade school kids. They are still growing at a rapid pace. However, there is a different view that I will get into in a later chapter.

Also avoid wind sprints at the beginning of practice. They require the loosest muscles, so they should normally be done at the end. Do short ones, 5 to 10 yards at first, then 25 yards. Tell the players to reach out in a long stride. Do some backward and sideways.

Finish with a few 25-yard races, linemen, ends and fullbacks, then backs.

Be creative! Set up an obstacle course of sprints, twenty-five push-ups, twenty-five sit-ups, a half-dozen somersault rollovers, more sprints. See who wins. Have a champion for each field position and encourage other players to beat his time. Set up relays. Make it fun and they won't groan so much!

You can't do much to make a slow kid a lot faster. But you can improve speed significantly, and you can improve running *strength*, agility and balance by a good deal.

Some good drills to improve running speed and form are:

1. *The Robot.* Line up the players and have them run 40 yards at half speed, alternatively driving their fists down from neck height to just behind the buttocks. The idea is to bang or hammer the fists downward in a robotic cadence in rhythm with their stride. Have them run it three times, increasing speed each time.

2. *The Bounce.* Similar to the drill above, except this time have them concentrate on lifting their knees high to the chest, bouncing off the ground with each step and lifting the knees as high as possible. Try to incorporate the first drill with the second after a while.

3. *The Buttkick.* Again run 40 yards and return, this time kicking the heels into the buttocks.

4. *The Goosestep.* Finally, run 40 yards in the old Russian or German military march, kicking the legs straight out and lifting them straight and high.

AGILITY DRILLS

1. *Simon Says.* Line up players in five lines. The first row of five start running in place, in short, quick, choppy steps. The coach signals the players to shuffle laterally (without crossing the feet), forward, backward, down to the ground and up again with his hand or a football in one hand. Players must square the shoulders, stay low and react quickly. Slow reacting play-

FIGURE 41
The Carioca

ers who don't appear to be trying hard enough may be rewarded with a dozen push-ups.
2. *Carioca.* Lined up as above, players carioca, that is, run sideways, left foot over right, then left foot behind right, for 40
   yards. Repeat four times. (See Figure 41.)
3. *Tire or Rope Drills.* These drills require a dozen or more old
   car tires, or 150 feet of rope and 100 feet of small PVC pipe
   with eight three-port three-dimensional couplings and eight
   to twelve T couplings.

   To use the tires, lay them in two off-center lines next to
   each other, and have players run through them, stepping
   through each hole. Time the players to see which group can
   go the fastest (linemen, ends, backs), and the competition will
   push them faster.

   If you use ropes, assemble the PVC into two rectangles 15
   to 20 feet by 8 feet. Connect these two structures at each corner
   and in two or three points along the long side by six or eight
   8″ to 10″ pipes. The height of these riser pipes can vary depending on the size of your team. The number you need along
   the long side should be enough to avoid sagging. PVC is cheap

and easy to cut. Attach and tape the rope so it forms two parallel rows of boxes; each box should be 18 inches long. Tell the players as they hop-step through it to stay low, lift the legs and stay balanced.

UNDERSTAND EACH PLAYER'S POTENTIAL

You need to figure out pretty quickly what each player can do, so each can concentrate on developing the specific skills for his position. Then you should keep an open mind, and figure out what players you were wrong about. I've seen many coaches assign positions quickly and then never change their mind. I offer a personal anecdote to dispute this attitude. I was an offensive end early in high school. One day my coach saw me knock a few players down and quickly moved me to what was my natural position, at tackle. While it's important to get things set early, so you can concentrate on the special skills required for each position (as discussed in chapter three), you should always be looking to see if a kid can better help the team somewhere else. Kids change from year to year, so don't base decisions exclusively on last year's performance. Assistant coaches can help you a lot here.

Make Lists

A good tool for understanding the potential of your players is to start making lists. Run sprints to see who your fastest players are. Rank and list them by speed for 40 yards. Who can accelerate the fastest (short distance speed)? Who are the most agile? Who are the gutsiest players? Who are the strongest players? Who has the best hands? Who are natural leaders? Make another list with each kid's name on it, and write down their best attributes. Once you create these lists, don't throw them away. Check them every couple of weeks, and see if someone has earned another look.

The lists are helpful since they focus you on different aspects of athletic ability. Periodically evaluate and reevaluate your players. It's incredible that some coaches rarely sit with assistant coaches and discuss each player. An assistant coach usually has seen something that can surface in such a full review. Don't just label someone for the season. Reconsider frequently. Give a kid a shot at something else if he is not working out where you first placed him.

You will find many brief opportunities on the practice field to talk to your players. How is school? How are things at home? What are your interests? You can find out a lot about a kid in just a few minutes to help you understand the player, and you will also begin to earn his respect. Kids who like and respect you are more coachable. You are a role model, so think about the messages you send by how you act.

WORK ON INDIVIDUAL SKILLS

After a half-hour of conditioning, stretching, speed and agility drills, call the players together. Tell them generally what they will be doing next and what you expect of them. Details can be supplied by assistant coaches later. Ask for their best effort on the field. You should now focus on skills and fundamentals for each position. I think it's a great idea to film kids at practice. Try to get parent volunteers to take some shots of players working on form, either blocking against the sled or dummy pads, running play patterns or pass catching. Do the linemen one day and the backs another. Circulate the tapes to kids who need to see what they are doing wrong. Perhaps the line coach or the backs coach can meet some of the players at someone's house to view the films and talk about form. In coaching a picture is truly worth a thousand words.

Linemen

Your linemen need to work repeatedly on their stance, charge and jolt, as well as on pulling and specialty blocks. After you (or the line coach) discuss with the players the fundamentals of blocking and tackling and demonstrate the correct form to them, have the players demonstrate the form back to you. (See Figure 42.) After they get it right, they are ready to perform the moves against other kids holding dummy pads. Have the checklist at the end of this book handy and see what needs to be adjusted. Make notes on each player so you and he know what changes need to be made in blocking form and work at them at each practice until the form

FIGURE 42
Mold the stance with each player until it is automatic for him.

FIGURE 43
Encourage them to pop the sled hard, low, and balanced.

is right. Then keep working on it to maintain good form. If the player knows about your list, and knows you will be looking at a specific part of his form at each practice, he will make it a priority. The concept of jolting can be practiced on dummies or on blocking sleds. Let kids know when they give the sled a good shot. Get everyone in the habit of trying to get the sled to jolt. Have everyone listen for the "pop" that accompanies a good charge and jolt. Go over the checklist. (See Figure 43.)

Too often I see assistant coaches standing around, saying or doing little. They should be looking at each player and insisting on proper form. Another tip: Some coaches fail to understand that some kids are reluctant to deliver a hard jolt against a friend or schoolmate. It makes sense to discuss this with the kids; tell them they must help each other out by understanding that it's not personal. They should expect to be hit hard, and should encourage teammates to go for it. They are a team! Bad habits should be avoided.

Working on form and fundamentals against dummy pads or sleds is essential. This must be done a few times a week. Good form goes a long way, If a head goes down, or the back curves, or if the legs stop driving or don't stay wide, let the player know. If he doesn't get the message, fifteen pushups will help him see your point. There is no excuse for poor form. A player may not be able to overcome an opponent, or execute every play well, but he can always employ proper form. Moreover, practice against sleds is the best method to strengthen legs and increase driving power.

Some of the best drills for linemen are done against a sled. If you have one available, it will help your players immensely. On sled drills you look for explosion, drive, jolt and follow-through, feet pumping all the time. Have the checklist handy to check out form. Agility can be added to the drill by having the players pop one pad, and roll off to pop the next pad. If you don't have access to a sled, use dummy pads or standing dummy bags. Two players holding one bag can put up a lot of resistance, and thus simulate the resistance of a sled.

Defensive linemen need some of the time to work on their fundamentals. They can work on the defensive stance, shivers, sheds and other defensive fundamentals while offensive linemen work on their form. However, *all* linemen should learn both offensive and defensive skills. As noted in chapter three, the defensive stance is a bit different. Also, linemen need to work on exploding off the snap, so have someone snapping the ball for timing drills. Have the coach who snaps the ball try to draw the defense offside by playing with the cadence. Have four or five linemen charge at each snap and see who gets off the fastest each time. Congratulate that player! Practice shiver thrusts against a sled or against dummy pads, and practice tackling against the sled or dummy bags. (See Figure 44.) Discuss the fundamentals of shedding. Review how to look for keys that tip off the offensive play.

I believe it's good to spend as much time as needed for practicing fundamentals and form. You should reserve about fifty minutes of a two and one-half hour practice for fundamentals. Twice a week you should spend twenty to thirty minutes in a live contact drill. In these drills, linemen are pitted against each other, one-on-one. Head to head, one blocks and the other tries to get around him.

FIGURE 44
Demonstrate the defensive *shiver* form against dummy pads.

FIGURE 45

One on one, man against man, contact drill. Talk to the players about their desire to overcome the opponent.

Set up cones so the defender can't just run laterally. The idea is to go through each other. Let each play go four to five seconds, then blow the whistle. This drill can be expanded to include a ballcarrier (who must stay within the cones). Remember, you are looking for *form* improvement as well as infusing the desire to overcome the opponent. Don't do more than two players at a time —you can then coach each player. Pit two offensive linemen, a yard apart, against a defensive lineman, who must go inbetween and through them. Practice pass blocking drills, one-on-one, two-on-two. (See Figure 45.)

Another good drill is one that anticipates defensive stunts. Take one side of the line (center-guard-tackle) against a noseguard-line-backer-tackle. Tell the players to move at full speed, but not full contact. Before each play the offense calls a play, in effect naming the hole the ball will go through (no ballcarrier is needed). The defense calls a stunt, or straight-on attack. The idea is to get the linemen thinking about how to react to the stunt in various situations.

Ends and Receivers

These players must share their time between pass-catching fundamentals and blocking. They work out with the linemen for a while, against the dummies or the sled on blocking form. They also work with the running backs (and defensive backs) on passing drills.

Ends are certainly called to take on defensive linemen head to head, and thus must work with other linemen on the charge and jolt. However, they are more often called upon to make an open field block on a linebacker or defensive back, so they need to work on specialty blocks such as cross-body blocks and downfield blocks. Downfield blocking is tough to do well, usually because it is not practiced enough. A good drill is to have two ends practice against each other. Line them up about 10 yards apart, and place a standing dummy bag between them, but about 10 yards to the side. One end must run and tackle the dummy, while the other tries to block him from it (stop the play a few seconds after contact is made). Adjust the players to equalize any speed advantage. You can employ a coach or a player with a pad to run wide and simulate the ballcarrier.

The other half of "fundamentals time" for ends is spent on running pass patterns. Ends need to work on controlling the defender. The best way, as stated in chapter two, is to run right at the defender and cut just when the defender changes his retreat. The end also needs to think about fakes. And, last but not least, he concentrates solely on the ball in flight and the receiving fundamentals. Part of the time should be spent just running patterns and catching passes, down and in, down and out, and deep patterns. He should be encouraged to pretend there is a defender on him, and go through fakes and sharp cuts. The other part of the time is spent with defensive backs who try to break the play up (no tackling, go for the ball only). Run actual pass plays without letting the defender know what the pattern is. It is essential to teach receivers to "see" the whole

FIGURE 46
THE PASSING TREE

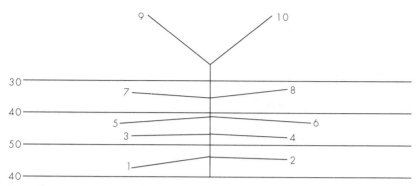

Legend: 1 and 2 = 6 yards and cut; 3 and 4 = 12 yards and cut; 5 and 6 = 18 yards andcut; 7 and 8 = 25 yards and cut; 9 and 10 = deep.

field, look for gaps, know where the defenders are.

Organizing the field into a passing tree helps to have everyone on the same page when practicing pass patterns. Different coaches use different trees; a typical passing tree is depicted in Figure 46.

Sometimes an end or wide receiver faces close coverage trying to stall him at the line. A good drill simulates this condition. The end should attack the defender, and then give him a head and shoulder fake. Don't let the defender get his hands into the body. Tell the receiver to push down on the defender's hands with one arm and use the other to swing free.

Beyond that, the idea is to catch a great number of passes. As in all sports, repetitions lead to perfection. Use two or three quarter-backs, use coaches, throwing to multiple lines of defenders, one line left, one right, one deep. At one point tell everyone to try to catch short passes with one hand. Rotate quarterbacks. One good drill is to place one receiver in a semicircle of four other receivers, with two footballs. He throws to one of the players in the semicircle, and another throws the second ball to him. He has to react quickly to be able to pass and catch both balls. After a while, another receiver goes to the middle.

Running Backs

Backs need to spend a lot of time with the quarterback practicing running patterns. They must perfect the handoff and work on their timing as the various running backs cross in front of each other or lead the ballcarrier. The first team should practice together. Coaches should focus on form and the other fundamentals listed in chapter three. Have your checklist handy and focus on each point. Look at the mechanics of the handoff: the position of outer and inner arms, the hands curled around the tips of the ball, the ball carried away from the nearest tackler. (See Figure 47.)

Running backs need to work with the ends on pass patterns and on pass-receiving fundamentals. They also need to work on blocking. Chapter three addressed open field blocking. A good drill for backs is the one mentioned above for ends. Use a moving dummy for the target.

A key for running backs is to protect the ball. At all levels of football, turnovers decide the game. Some time *must* be spent every week on ball security. A good drill is to have the quarterback simulate a snap and then hand off to a running back. A few yards away, position two players (two other running backs) with dummy pads. Their job is to jolt the running back with the pads just after he gets the ball and use a free hand to try to strip the ball. The runner must go *between* the two players. This can also be done with a gauntlet of players with dummies, all trying to strip the ball.

Backs should also practice switching the ball from one arm to the other, to move it opposite from the nearest tackler. A good drill is the *slalom*: Have six or more backs line up in a zigzag pattern. One back with the ball slaloms past these backs, switching the ball from arm to arm as he approaches each player (he should nudge each player). The defending players take a swipe at the ball (not the runner). Then the runner takes his position at the end of the pattern, and the first back in the pattern takes a shot at the slalom. Run it until each player gets several turns.

Quarterbacks

The quarterback and center should take a few dozen snaps a day, over and above the snaps during drills. They can't get enough of this routine, and anyone experienced with youth football knows how often the ball is lost on bad snaps. The players will get bored with it all, but it must be practiced. Have a dummy line up opposite the center and give the center a jolt with the pad upon the snap. *Always* have the quarterback drop back or pivot when practicing snaps, as it makes no sense to practice a stationary snap that will never occur in a game. A good diagnostic drill is to have the quarterback take snaps with only his top hand. If the ball falls straight down without turning or spinning, the snap is good. Quarterbacks should be encouraged to spend a lot of time fooling with the ball. A quarterback should always have a ball in his hands. Spin it up into the air; drop it and catch it with one hand; juggle it; exchange it behind the back, between the legs. I remember Phil Simms, formerly of the Giants, doing this constantly on the sidelines. Quarterbacks need to squeeze tennis balls, and perform other exercises to strengthen their wrists. They should practice passing while on the run, jumping, on one knee, and on their backs. Quarterbacks should practice the three, five and seven step drop, always retreating quickly, as well as throwing with the nose up (for long passes) and with it even or down a bit (for short passes). Check their grip of the ball, and adjust it if needed.

Specialty Practice

The punter and the field goal kicker must work with the center on long snaps. Your starting receiver needs to practice receptions. Remember the fundamentals, and keep your checklist handy. Don't take specialty teamwork for granted as this is often where mistakes are made. Kickoffs, punts and field goals all need to be practiced at least once a week. The day before a game is the best time.

WORK ON TEAM EXECUTION OF PLAYS

Individual skills and proper form must come together like clockwork on the field. The offense *must* spend a considerable portion of practice time on running plays. Live contact scrimmage is of course the most effective way to accomplish this, but it is also a good way to increase injuries. I would not scrimmage the offense more than once a week, and I never allow tackling the quarterback on pass plays; two-hand touch is the limit.

You can conduct dummy scrimmages by running plays against a defense with dummy pads. Tell the defenders to try to knock down the ballcarrier with the pads while running. Stop the play when a defender makes good contact with a pad. On passing plays, tell the pass defense to drop the pads and play for the ball only. Run a play until everyone gets it right.

Live scrimmages are usually held midweek. This gives players a day or two to get over any soreness before the weekend game. Keep your eye on the matchups, so no one is seriously overmatched and gets repeatedly belted. The players are well padded, but make sure you try to reduce the possibility of injury, particularly at grade school levels.

THE PRACTICE PLAN

Each practice should have a written practice plan. I've developed a form that's on the last page of this chapter. Make a few dozen copies of it, and fill it out for each practice. You can double the value of the practice if you are well organized.

Your practice plans should vary over the course of the season. The focus of the first weeks of practice in the fall season is conditioning and deciding what positions should be assigned to each player. After a few weeks, as games approach, focus shifts to individual skills, and then to team dynamics. *All of these elements, however, should be part of the plan in every week's practice all year.*

Monday

TIME ACTIVITY

5:30 P.M. **CONDITIONING:** Whole team run one lap. Line up team in rows by position. Do Cali Set. Do Stretch Set.

SPEED DRILLS: Robot, Bounce, Buttkick, Goosestep.

AGILITY DRILLS: Simon Says, Carioca, Tire Drill.

5:55 P.M. **CALL TEAM TOGETHER.** Brief comments.

6:00 P.M. **FUNDAMENTALS:** Three groups: linemen, backs, receivers.

LINEMEN AND ENDS: 1) Review stance and set position form. 2) Practice charge and jolt form against dummy pads.

BACKS: 1) Review form of stance, pivot and step; QB practices form for drop steps. 2) Practice handoff mechanics. 3) Do running patterns.

6:30 P.M. **WATER BREAK.**

6:40 P.M. **CONTINUE FUNDAMENTALS: LINEMEN:** Practice defensive shiver against dummy pads.

BACKS AND ENDS: Pass practice lines, use the whole passing tree.

7:00 P.M. **TEAM PRACTICE:** Run offensive plays against dummies. Punter and placekicker work 20 minutes on kicks, other end of field.

7:50 P.M. **WIND SPRINTS,** by position.

8:00 P.M. **CLOSING COMMENTS,** practice over.

Tuesday

TIME ACTIVITY

5:30 P.M. **CONDITIONING:** Whole team run one lap. Line up team in rows by position. Do Cali Set. Do Stretch Set.

SPEED DRILLS: Robot, Bounce, Buttkick, Goosestep.

AGILITY DRILLS: Simon Says, Carioca, Tire Drill.

5:55 P.M. **CALL TEAM TOGETHER.** Brief comments.

6:00 P.M. **FUNDAMENTALS:** Three groups: linemen, backs, receivers.

LINEMEN AND ENDS: 1) Do timing drill for defensive charge on center snap. 2) Practice charge, jolt and drive on sled.

BACKS: 1) Ball security drills using dummies who swipe at the ball. 2) Practice running patterns.

6:30 P.M.   **WATER BREAK.**

6:40 P.M.   **CONTINUE FUNDAMENTALS: LINEMEN:** Practice tackling form against dummy bags.

BACKS AND ENDS: Practice downfield blocking on dummy pads.

7:00 P.M.   **TEAM PRACTICE:** 1) Run offensive plays against dummies, 30 minutes. 2) First team defense practices stunts and reaction against offense, low contact. Punter and placekicker work 20 minutes on kicks, other end of field.

7:50 P.M.   **WIND SPRINTS,** by position.

8:00 P.M.   **CLOSING COMMENTS,** practice over.

Wednesday

TIME   ACTIVITY

5:30 P.M.   **CONDITIONING:** Whole team run one lap. Line up team in rows by position. Do Cali Set. Do Stretch Set.

SPEED DRILLS: Robot, Bounce, Buttkick, Goosestep.

AGILITY DRILLS: Simon Says, Carioca, Tire Drill.

5:55 P.M.   **CALL TEAM TOGETHER.** Brief comments

6:00 P.M.   **FUNDAMENTALS:** Three groups: linemen, backs, receivers.

LINEMEN: 1) Review ways to detect tipoffs and other keys from offensive players. 2) Practice pulling mechanics. 3) Practice crab blocks.

BACKS AND ENDS: 1) Practice form for open-field tackling. 2) Practice shedding downfield blockers.

6:30 P.M.   **WATER BREAK.**

6:40 P.M.   **CONTINUE FUNDAMENTALS: LINEMEN AND ENDS:** One-on-one full contact blocking. **BACKS:** 1) Run offensive play patterns. 2) Ball security drills.

7:00 P.M.   **TEAM PRACTICE:** Offensive scrimmage. Full contact.

7:50 P.M.   **WIND SPRINTS,** by position.

8:00 P.M.   **CLOSING COMMENTS,** practice over.

Thursday

TIME	ACTIVITY
5:30 P.M.	**CONDITIONING:** Whole team run one lap. Line up team in rows by position. Do Cali Set. Do Stretch Set.
	SPEED DRILLS: Robot, Bounce, Buttkick, Goosestep.
	AGILITY DRILLS: Simon Says, Carioca, Tire Drill.
5:55 P.M.	**CALL TEAM TOGETHER.** Brief comments.
6:00 P.M.	**FUNDAMENTALS:** Three groups: linemen, backs and receivers.
	LINEMEN AND ENDS: 1) Downfield blocking. 2) Defensive shed methods.
	BACKS: 1)Blocking form on sled. 2) Tackling form on dummy bags.
6:30 P.M.	**WATER BREAK.**
6:40 P.M.	**CONTINUE FUNDAMENTALS: LINEMEN:** Charge, jolt and drive on sled.
	BACKS AND ENDS: Pass practice lines, use the whole passing tree.
7:00 P.M.	**TEAM PRACTICE:** 1) Defensive scrimmage (30 minutes). 2) Punts and returns. Punter and placekicker work 20 minutes on kicks, other end of field, during scrimmage.
7:50 P.M.	**WIND SPRINTS,** by position.
8:00 P.M.	**CLOSING COMMENTS,** practice over.

Friday

TIME	ACTIVITY
5:30 P.M.	**CONDITIONING:** Run one lap, do Cali Set, do Stretch Set. Run one lap.
5:45 P.M.	**CALL TEAM TOGETHER.** Brief comments.
5:50 P.M.	**RUN OFFENSIVE PATTERNS.**
6:10 P.M.	**PUNTS AND RETURNS.**
6:40 P.M.	**KICKOFFS AND RETURNS.**
7:10 P.M.	**PLACEKICKING AND DEFENSE.**
7:30 P.M.	**CLOSING COMMENTS:** practice over.

DAILY PRACTICE SCHEDULE

Day

TIME   ACTIVITY

_____   _____

_____   _____

_____   _____

_____   _____

_____   _____

_____   _____

_____   _____

_____   _____

_____   _____

_____   _____

_____   _____

_____   _____

_____   _____

_____   _____

Chapter Eight

A YOUNG ATHLETE'S HEALTH

You can do only so much to improve athletic ability, but you can do a great deal to maintain good health. Football is a rugged contact sport, and a healthy body goes a long way toward better performance on the field and avoiding injury.

DIET

Obviously, a balanced diet is essential. There are many books on diet, and your doctor, school nurse or team trainer can also advise you. Good nutrition helps develop strength, endurance and concentration. A good diet balances proteins, carbohydrates and fats. An athlete in training needs mainly complex carbohydrates, at least 70 percent of the total diet, with fats (10 percent) and proteins (20 percent) splitting the remainder. Popular today is the *food guide pyramid*. (See Figure 48). Complex carbohydrates dominate the base grouping, calling for greater doses of breads, cereal, rice and pasta. Vegetables and fruits respectively take up the next level, calling for a few daily servings each. The dairy group and the meat, fish and poultry group are next, with fats last.

Early in the season, particularly during double sessions in the heat at the end of the summer, a dinner high in carbohydrates helps maintain energy the next day. Pasta is the best meal for this. A banana each day during this intensive period helps prevent potassium depletion. Complex carbohydrates are the primary source of fuel and energy for the athlete. They are broken down into glucose, the body's main source of energy. What is not needed is stored for future use. Avoid simple carbohydrates such as sugar and honey. The old adage that a candy bar just before a game gives an energy boost is misleading since simple carbohydrates cause unstable supplies of glucose (ever notice how tired you feel after a sweets overload?). Good sources of complex carbohydrates are corn on the cob, wild rice, brown rice, whole wheat and whole rye.

FIGURE 48

THE FOOD GUIDE PYRAMID

A guide to Daily Food Choices

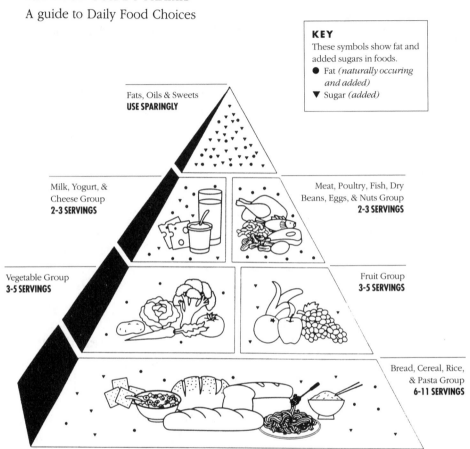

KEY

These symbols show fat and added sugars in foods.

● Fat *(naturally occuring and added)*

▼ Sugar *(added)*

Fats, Oils & Sweets
USE SPARINGLY

Milk, Yogurt, &
Cheese Group
2-3 SERVINGS

Meat, Poultry, Fish, Dry
Beans, Eggs, & Nuts Group
2-3 SERVINGS

Vegetable Group
3-5 SERVINGS

Fruit Group
3-5 SERVINGS

Bread, Cereal, Rice,
& Pasta Group
6-11 SERVINGS

The pyramid is an outline of what to eat each day. It's not a rigid prescription, but a general guide that lets you choose a healthful diet that's right for you. The Pyramid calls for eating a variety of foods to get the nutrients you need and at the same time the right amount of calories to maintain a healthy weight.

A Typical High-Carbohydrate Diet
Breakfast

- 8 oz. orange juice or a grapefruit or 8 oz. apple juice
- Bowl shredded wheat (low-fat milk) or oatmeal or cream of farina
- (a) Bacon and two eggs or (b) pancakes and butter
- Several slices of whole wheat toast and butter
- Daily vitamin, adult dosage
- 10 oz. water

Lunch

- 1 bowl of soup: chicken, clam chowder or vegetable
- 2 pieces broiled chicken or 6 oz. broiled fish
- Green salad with oil and vinegar
- Cooked rice or a potato (no french fries)
- 2 slices of enriched bread
- 12 to 16 oz. milk
- 10 oz. water

Dinner

- 1 bowl of soup: cream of mushroom, cream of potato, or vegetable.
- Linguine with tomato or clam sauce
- Baked potato
- Cooked vegetable: corn, broccoli, peas or beans
- Beverage of choice
- 10 oz. water

Desserts or Snacks

- Bananas, apples, raisins, strawberries, melons
- 10 oz. water

Water

Most teams allow water breaks, so make sure each player has a water bottle. Midpractice is not a good time to load up on water, so tell players to limit themselves to a cup at each break. He needs a couple of quarts a day, or more if it's hot outside early in the season. It's a good habit to drink plenty of water, so be sure he has some at each meal. It is also important to drink plenty of fluids before, during and after practices. Dehydration reduces performance and can lead to serious medical problems.

Alcohol, Tobacco and Drugs

Alcohol, tobacco and drugs have effects we are all too aware of. They destroy lives and can even kill. Kids are getting this message now. What young players may not think about enough is that these substances substantially reduce their playing performance—and reduced performance can put your son out of the running for a starting position, or even for making the team. Be sure to discuss this practical concern.

Sleep

Sufficient sleep is also a concern. A player starts the season with double sessions of practice, so you won't have to worry too much at first, since he will come right home and hit the pillow. However, into the season, particularly at high school levels, he may try to burn the candle at both ends. Again, I find that kids relate better when they consider practical consequences of their actions. Lack of sufficient rest diminishes performance. Diminished performance costs him playing time.

CONDITIONING, STRENGTH TRAINING, WEIGHTS

Kids should be encouraged to do some conditioning in the off-season. Until high school varsity level play, a good program of calisthenics is adequate. Football requires more strength than most sports. It is not, however, an endurance sport, and kids can always find a moment to take a breather. Most coaches concentrate on improving strength and toughness. Of course, jogging won't hurt conditioning, but it may take away needed weight. Wind sprints are much better and it never hurts to add them to training sessions.

I will get into weight training below, but I don't encourage it for grade school players. A good calisthenic program that works on legs and upper body is adequate.

1. Push-ups are a great exercise since upper body strength is so important to football, and they can be done anytime, anywhere. A player should do fifty to one hundred per day. He will spend most of his time shoving another kid around, and the one with the strongest chest and shoulders will prevail. The upper body gets a better workout if the hands are elevated six inches, on some books or a block, so the chest can descend a few inches lower.

2. Pull-ups are also quite helpful. These are chin-ups with the hands reversed and spread as wide as possible. Again, upper body strength is crucial and any help that you can give here will be immediately and quite noticeably rewarded on the field. I got my son a set of chest expanders, with springs attached to handles, and he used them while watching his silly cartoons.

3. Partial sit-ups are great for strengthening the midsection. Lie on the back, knees bent, and lift the shoulder blades off the floor.

4. Dips are popular and great for the upper body. They require parallel bars. The idea is to dip the body so the arms are bent at least ninety degrees, then push up, straightening the arms. A single bar can be used for back dips, holding the bar behind the back, dipping to ninety degrees and pushing back up.

5. Rowing exercises are also very good for increasing strength and stamina.

6. Next, and perhaps most important in football, come the legs. Partial squats, bending the knee halfway with some extra weight added, are quite good. Don't bend all the way.

7. The longstanding tradition of running up stairs is excellent.

8. A nice leg strengthener is the *lunge*. The idea is to step forward and dip until the back leg bends to a ninety-degree angle, then push away from the floor and straighten the legs.

9. Gentle neck exercises are also good, since the neck takes a pounding. Neck bridges are probably the best, but be careful not to overdo it here. Perhaps you can get a few pillows under the back to reduce the strain initially.

Muscles are like bubble gum. If you stretch gum quickly, it tears or snaps, but if you stretch it slowly it expands nicely. Stretching before training, practice or games helps prevent muscles from tearing or snapping. No practice of any kind should begin without some slow jogging, some jumping jacks (for the ankles), and some general stretching (for the upper thigh, trunk and neck). Running sideways and backward or any agility exercises are quite good also. See the exercises recommended for practices in the previous chapter.

WEIGHT TRAINING

When I wrote the first edition of this book, I was clear that weight training should be avoided by grade school level players and not started until mid-high-school years. Part of the reason was intuitive: A child's body is growing rapidly until then. I was also aware of some studies done in the 1970s that showed that grade school kids do not gain much strength from weight lifting due to low levels of male hormones. These studies also suggested that there was significant risk of injury to the kid's growth plates, which are the ends of the long bones that account for growth.

A careful study of 354 high school football players, reported in 1990 by Dr. William Risser of the University of Texas Medical School, found that weight lifting can cause severe musculoskeletal injuries, usually muscle strains and often in the lower back. In the study, 7.1 percent of the players reported injury. Injuries occurred when free weights were used in major lifts such as the clean and jerk, the snatch, the squat lift, the dead lift, the power clean, and the bench, incline and overhead press. Injury often occurred in the home and was related to poor technique and form, lack of warmup, and lack of a spotter to assist.

I'm still against kids lifting weights, but I must report that more recent research suggests a different point of view. In the November 1990 issue of *Pediatrics* (Vol. 86, No. 5), the American Academy of Pediatrics Committee on Sports Medicine states that "Recent research has shown that short-term programs in which prepubescent [grade school] athletes are trained and supervised by knowledgeable adults can increase strength without significant injury risk." The statement went on to say:

Interscholastic athletic programs in secondary schools are increasingly emphasizing strength training as a conditioning method for participants in male and female sports. The major lifts are often used . . . Strength training in adolescence occasionally produces significant musculoskeletal injury . . . especially during use of the major lifts. Safety requires careful planning of several aspects of a program. This includes devising a program for the intensity, duration, frequency, and rate of progression of weight use, as well as selection of sport-specific exercises appropriate for the physical maturity of the individual. Proper supervision should be provided during training sessions.

The committee also addressed the issue of when kids should be allowed to lift maximal amounts of weight, that is, the greatest amount of weight they can successfully lift. They concluded this should be avoided until they have passed their period of maximal velocity of height growth. Young people reach that stage *on average* at age fifteen; however, the committee also notes that there is "much individual variation." Consequently, based on the contents of this article, the American Academy of Pediatrics recommends that each child's stage of physical maturity be assessed by medical personnel and that the adults planning strength training programs be qualified to develop programs appropriate for varying stages of maturity.

Another excellent article, "Strength Training in Children and Adolescents" (*Pediatric Clinics of North America*, October 1990), was written by Dr. David Webb at the Center for Sportsmedicine, Saint Francis Memorial Hospital, San Francisco, California. He found that most injuries occurred in the home and were unsupervised and that there is not an inordinate risk of injury in weight training if it's properly done. He also reported that strength training can help kids excel in sports, and that it can actually *reduce* the incidence of muscle or tendon injuries in sports.

What does this all mean? Knowledgeable trainers can help a

player gain strength at all levels of play and weight training helps young football players. Since most kids are urged to do it, those who don't will be at a disadvantage. However, any program should avoid maximal weight lifts until the mid-high-school years. Be careful; injury can still occur no matter what.

Let's face it. Anyone who has ever lifted weights knows that, even if you follow a good program, kids have a powerful urge to finish with some heavy weights, to see how much they can lift. If unsupervised, they will go for the max at some point. This is one of the main reasons I frown on the idea. I also resent the idea that we should heighten the competitive pressure of athletics in grade school by creating a need to strength train in order to "keep up." But the reality is that at the high school level players need to do weights if they are to be competitive. As a parent you must ensure that they are supervised, and that they follow a sound program. A 7 percent injury rate is quite high, so parents must assert controls on this matter.

If a player undertakes a weight training program, as advised above, he should have the supervision and advice of a knowledgeable trainer. Parents should ask their doctor if their son has any preexisting health conditions that can be aggravated by such training. High blood pressure is one condition that doesn't mix with weights. Any pain should be reported to the trainer. Warmup and stretching exercises should be done before lifting. Lifting maximal weights or engaging in *ballistic* sudden jerking exercises such as clean and jerk should not be done. Kids should generally use weights that can be done in sets of fifteen repetitions. They should not lift every day, but every other day at the most. All major muscle groups should get some attention to keep development balanced, although the emphasis in football is on the legs.

In the weight room, football players should emphasize heavy leg exercises. Squats are best because leg strength is of primary importance. The equipment for this should include a squat stand that holds the barbell. The player squats with the barbell on his shoulders to a height that requires his upper and lower legs to form a ninety-degree angle. He should not go lower unless he can

FIGURE 49

This is the deadliest play in football: head down, blocking with the top of the helmet!

maintain good form, straight back, balanced feet. He should *always* have a spotter.

Proper tackling starts with the legs, which are also to be conditioned with sets of hamstring curls, leg extenders and leg presses. The program should also include sets of upright rows, incline bench presses, lat pull downs, and dumbbell shoulder presses. The trainer should explain how to do these and other exercises.

INJURIES

As mentioned earlier, football equipment today is vastly improved. Moreover, at grade school levels, the kids are smaller and don't hit with the force of older, heavier players. Also, kids are usually quite resilient. Yet football is a full contact sport, and injuries occur. There are things parents can do to reduce the probability of injury and to avoid seriously compounding an injury that does occur.

The first thing parents and coaches should do is personally educate their players about the dangers of *spearing*—using the helmet to deliver a blow, either blocking, tackling, or running with the ball. Spearing is illegal, and is the most dangerous act in all of football. I'll discuss brain and spinal injuries in more detail later in this chapter. It's also useful to chat with the coach about this. Coaches usually are fully aware of this, and coach kids to keep their heads up, but it never hurts to increase a coach's sensitivity to this problem. (See Figure 49.)

Another step is to inspect equipment. Is the helmet padding intact? Does it fit properly? Are the chin straps snug? Are they frayed? Is the mouthpiece attached to the helmet? Does it fit? Are the shoulder pad straps and laces snug? Are hip, thigh and tailbone pads in good shape? Are the knee pads OK?

How about the practice fields? Are there any stones or other protrusions? Are there any holes, ruts or tracks (this is how ankles get sprained)? If you see any, let the coach know so he can avoid them. Perhaps you can get a few other parents together to fill any holes or remove any protrusions or other debris.

Finally, is there a trainer or someone qualified in first aid at practice? This is *very* important during days the players scrimmage or otherwise engage in full body contact. Most leagues require coaches to obtain licenses that expose them to first aid techniques, but is there someone who really knows what to do? If not, remember that parents can take a course and become quite knowledgeable. Perhaps a parent can volunteer as a trainer.

I watched a team scrimmage just a few days before I wrote this chapter. A kid twisted his knee. The coach was shorthanded for players, and seemed more concerned about getting the kid back into the scrimmage than worrying about the extent of any injury. A few minutes later the kid was back in the action, and after a play I noticed he was limping a bit. The coach never looked at him! As a parent, it pays to attend a few practices to see how sensitive the coach is to injury. A good rule is that a player who complains of any injury to any joint cannot play for at least ten minutes to see if pain or swelling is still present.

No matter how well conditioned a team is, injuries can occur anytime. A common injury is a hamstring pull, but this usually doesn't occur until high school or later. Strained knees, ankles and necks are the most common to football. Upper leg (groin) strains, bloody noses, sprained wrists and forearms, jammed fingers, dislocations and bruises also occur. Thankfully, broken bones are rare. Most youth teams have trained first-aid people. I went through the program for my son's team and it was quite useful. Ambulances are usually present at games, but not at practices, where many injuries occur.

Abrasions occur often on the nose, although modern face gear protects the face much better than when I played. They also show up on the elbow, forearm and lower leg. These cuts are the most likely to get infected. Wash the wound as soon as possible, with soap if it is handy. Apply a dressing when you can—the sooner the better! Put some antiseptic on it. If it gets red or oozes pus, see a physician.

Lacerations are deeper wounds. Unless bleeding is severe, wash the wound and apply direct pressure with a bandage to stop the bleeding. If severe or deep, seek first aid. Keep applying pressure and secure the dressing with a bandage (you can tie the knot right over the wound to reinforce the pressure). Immediately elevate the wound higher than the heart to help slow the bleeding. Remember, if the bandage over the wound gets blood soaked, don't remove it; just apply a new dressing right over it. If the person has lost a lot of blood, you'll need to treat him for shock. Keep him warm with blankets and call for help. If a laceration is major, a butterfly bandage will hold the skin together. Consult a physician immediately for stitches.

Contusions and bruises occur frequently. Apply ice quickly after taking care of any abrasions or lacerations. Ice arrests internal bleeding and prevents or lessens swelling. Ice is the best first aid available for nearly any swelling from bruises or sprains. Apply it very quickly. Do not move the child, especially if he is down due to a tough tackle or jolt. He could have a spinal injury and the slightest movement by an untrained person could do some serious damage.

Sprained ankles, knees and wrists should be immobilized. An ice pack should be applied immediately. Act as if there is a fracture until you're sure there isn't. Call an ambulance if there is any question in your mind. Get an x-ray to see if there is a break or other damage.

If there is a fracture, immobilize the child completely as soon as possible. There should be no movement at all. Comfort him, warm him with coats or blankets, and get medical help. Do not allow a child to be moved or cared for by anyone who is not medically trained. If he is in the middle of the field during a championship game, the game can wait. Insist on this. Permanent damage can result from aggravating a break.

Finally, heat exhaustion can occur during football practices or games, particularly early in the season during those sweltering August practice sessions. The body gets clammy and pale. Remove the child from the playing field, apply cool towels and elevate the feet. If the body temperature is very high and pupils are contracted, you should suspect heat stroke. Call an ambulance and cool him down fast. Treat for shock.

Knees are tough injuries. Often the injury requires some sort of arthroscopic surgery to mend cartilage. Modern procedures are quite advanced and simple. Have a child see a knowledgeable sports doctor. Your team's coach or high school athletic director will know one.

Tell players to play the game safely. Aggressiveness is okay, but he should never intentionally hurt someone. I play flag football frequently, and there are often one or two guys who take chances with the health of others. Don't encourage a child to grow up like them.

When an injury occurs, insist on rest. I've seen many kids rush back from a sprained ankle, only to have the injury plague them through the years. Don't let it happen! And make sure that a player wears an ankle brace from then on. There are excellent ankle braces on the market today.

The point is that injuries need time to heal right. If you give them that time, the future can have many years of sports for each player. If you don't, his playing days could be over already.

Critical Injuries

If a child ever falls to the ground unconscious, see if anyone present has been trained in first aid. Once it is clear that the child does not respond, the first move is to check for the vital signs: airway, breathing and circulation, the ABCs of first aid. Send for an ambulance and let a trained person administer rescue breathing or CPR (cardiopulmonary resuscitation), if necessary. Try to stay calm and let the first-aiders do their job. In all my years of coaching four sports and playing even more, I've never seen CPR needed. I hope that you won't either.

Catastrophic spine and brain injuries among football players are rare and have decreased more in the past twenty years with improvements to equipment and with rules against head spearing. Yet they do happen. This is obviously a most unpleasant subject, but it is important that you understand some of the detail because many deadly injuries of the brain and paralyzing injuries of the spine are caused by earlier blows. A concerned and informed parent or coach could step in and prevent serious injury.

Many fans will recall the awful TV image of Dennis Byrd of the New York Jets severely injuring himself by smashing headfirst into teammate Scott Mersereau's chest as they both attempted to tackle Kansas City Chief's quarterback Dave Krieg. The image reminded me of a similar play nearly thirty years ago as I dove toward a running back at the line of scrimmage and collided headfirst with my own linebacker as the running back put on a spurt past us. It was the hardest blow I ever took, and I remember thinking that the lights would go out. I groggily got up and was able to collect myself. Fortunately, there was a penalty on the play, so I had time to figure out who and where I was. The linebacker was in the same state I was. I continued to play, but I should have been taken off the field.

While the neck is relatively fragile, the neck muscles are quite strong and generally absorb the shock of most blows. With the head up, the upper shoulder muscles and upper back help out. However, when a blow or jolt is taken by the top of the head (helmet), it goes down the spine, compresses the discs, and forces them to buckle. The spinal cord is like a rope made of millions of small strands carrying the information of the central nervous system. When this is bruised or damaged by the buckling spinal sheath, it's like a broken TV cable . . . no signal!

These injuries are reported by the National Collegiate Athletic Association (NCAA) survey of catastrophic football injuries. They occurred about twenty times a year nationwide in college and high school in the early 1970s. However, with improvements in equipment, bans on spearing, and better conditioning of the neck muscles, the incidence of permanent cervical spinal cord injury has been cut in half and is a bit more than one in two hundred thousand. Such injuries are even rarer at the grade school level. Most of these injuries occur to defensive players during tackling or to those on kickoff teams.

This is not to say that every neck strain is a major injury. A fairly common injury is known as a *burner*. A group of physicians discussed this injury in the September, 1991, issue of *The Physician and Sportsmedicine*. Burners are a temporary nerve dysfunction caused by a blow to the neck, head or shoulder. They are like pinched nerves and arise from a sudden stretching of nerve channels. The player experiences a sharp pain—it can seem like an electric shock—followed by a burning sensation. The sensation can radiate down the arm, and can be accompanied by sharp reflex action. I know about burners because I had one in practice one day, going one-on-one with a big lineman. It felt like a buzzing in my lower neck and pain in my left arm. I had some occasional soreness there for years, especially after a lot of exercise. Burners usually go away, sometimes after a few minutes. However, players should *always* see a physician, and certainly should get a neck collar. Now that you know the symptoms, take control if it happens.

More serious than spinal injuries are possible injury to the head and brain. The *Journal of the American Medical Association* (JAMA) reported in 1991 on a University of Colorado School of Medicine study of players who died after receiving head blows where the fatal injury was actually caused by an earlier head blow. Thus, a player can receive a concussion, never black out, and that brain swelling then can become lethal days later, triggered by a relatively minor blow. *Any* level of confusion or headache brought on by a blow to the head should receive *immediate* medical attention. Get the player out of the game! The Colorado Medical Society recommends that players who sustain a severe blow to the head be removed for at least twenty minutes, and not be allowed to return to the game if any confusion or amnesia persists during that time. If a player ever loses consciousness, he should go straight to the hospital.

Chapter Nine

FINAL THOUGHTS

WORK WITH YOUR CHILD

Parents and coaches should honestly evaluate a player's potential and desire. If he is a beginner, then the first objective is to learn the game fundamentals. Go over terminology and concepts. Talk about desire: the determination to overcome an opponent. Review the basic skill concepts behind blocking and tackling. Take him to a high school, college or pro game.

Start by promoting a good diet, and then focus on conditioning. Get some advice on what position seems best suited for him and evaluate his speed. Encourage him to go out with his friends and play two-hand touch games. (In two-hand touch a player is down when a defender touches him with both hands.) Kids like to play tackle football, but without protective equipment, it makes no sense. Many youth leagues have flag football for the very young ages, and it is good experience to learn some fundamentals. If your town has a flag league, get him to try out.

Review the main offensive and defensive concepts. Talk about each of the various positions. A local high school game is a great place to sit and review the fundamentals, watching as they actually occur in front of you.

As he becomes a decent player, parents can help by concentrating on specific skills. If he is tall, give him practice receiving passes while someone defends, but only aggressively enough to make it a challenge. Take some video shots (zoom in to the maximum) of his play, and review the videotape with him. Don't be too critical! Let him evaluate his own performance.

I think it's most important to try to keep the game in perspective. It's easy to associate this sport with overly aggressive behavior. That can be most unfortunate, particularly if it turns him into a bully.

Try to emphasize the positive aspects—the character building, the development of courage, and the growth of team spirit. In life we often get knocked down and then rise again to achieve. Football teaches life lessons. Discourage the degrading aspects.

BOYS AND GIRLS

I have no problem with girls playing football. Any athlete who can perform has a clear right to do so in my judgment, and this right is protected under federal law and in most states. At very young ages girls and boys are very close in speed and aggressiveness and much closer in strength than in later years. At this level girls can clearly play the game. They rarely do. Perhaps this is in recognition that there is little future for them in the game. All-girl teams in high school are unheard of. Also, as I noted earlier, football is less about the precision skills that girls can achieve and more about sheer strength, which Mother Nature has not given to many of them. Upper body strength is essential, and few girls have it.

While I would not recommend that you encourage football as a choice for a young girl, she should never be denied the chance to try it. If she is gifted and determined, particularly at a young age, why not? I admire the girls who have done it under great media pressure, and perhaps someday it will grow as a women's sport. I believe more women will play; however, I doubt it will grow much.

An article in the September 1993 issue of *NEA Today* had two high school coaches debating the pros and cons of women in football. Presenting the opposing view, a coach from Texas noted the sheer physical strength differences between boys and girls, problems with insurance, increased cost for separate facilities for girls at practices and games, and an increased likelihood of injury. The Utah coach arguing in favor of the idea had a girl on his team, with no problems. He said she added a lot to the team and was accepted as "one of the guys." She kicked conversions and caught passes. It was no problem getting a room for her to dress. He did note, however, that the guys took it a bit easy on her, and I worry about the higher injury potential in games for a player who isn't toughened up properly and challenged fully at practices.

About one hundred girls play high school football each year across the country. It's been about a quarter of a century since Congress passed Title IX of the Education Amendments of 1972, the federal legislation that bans sex discrimination in schools receiving federal funds and requires schools to provide equal sports opportunities for males and females. As a result, the participation of women in sports at the high school level has increased sevenfold during that time—to nearly two million today. Colleges have increased the share of money going to women's sports but have a long way to go since men's programs still get nearly three times the money.

Nevertheless, the pioneers of women's football have set the precedent and paved the way. It may be that the media and critics of women in football have focused too much on players, such as Tawana Hammonds, a female high-school player in Maryland whose internal injuries cost her a spleen and half her pancreas. She later sued her school's board of education for not properly informing her of the inherent risks of playing football. But this scenario should not diminish the accomplishment of the many hundreds of others who had a great experience with the game, players like Sally Phillips of Spanish River, Florida, a placekicker who was crowned homecoming queen while wearing full football gear because she had no time to dress after practice. Split end Sarah Price of Chamblee, Georgia, had the most uncommon experience of playing head to head against cornerback April Smith of Seneca, South Carolina. In 1989, two women, tight end Sabrina Wells and defensive back Lakeal Ellis, both played in the Washington, D.C., area and earned the respect of players and coaches. In 1985 Carol White became the nation's first major collegiate female football coach at Georgia Tech, working with punters and placekickers.

The opportunity exists. If a girl wants to play the game, she should start at the grade school level. The competition will be more even, and she will have a chance to see what potential is there.

Some high schools or leagues have flag football. This sport focuses more on skill and speed than strength and is certainly suited for women as well as for men. In flag football, players wear a belt with two long yellow ribbons attached by Velcro to the belt at each hip. A player is "tackled" when a defender grabs and pulls one of the ribbons or "flags" from the belt. Rules can require that both flags be pulled away, and this makes for a more physical game. Teams usually field six to eight players. It's basically a passing game, and some rules allow only passing. Most players run pass patterns while one or two stay back to block for the quarterback. Fields are usually 50 yards long, but this varies greatly. When I was about thirty, we set up a flag league in my townhouse association. About eighty guys and some women showed up. After the first two weeks there were twenty left, the rest having been sidelined by dozens of sprains and strains (one broken finger).

Some high schools have *powder-puff*, a flag football variant, games for girls, but in many towns it's just a fun game, and often guys dress up as girls to join in.

ADVICE FOR PARENTS IN THE STANDS

Football stands are loud places. The game seems to fire up everyone and so you will have to go with the flow. The noise is part of it all. Unfortunately, there are always a few superscreamers—parents who get out of control. They look quite foolish and are very irritating to sit near. It is as if they have been given a license to leave their senses. Sure, everyone cheers loudly on a big play, but don't be a spectacle. Have some consideration for the fans around you.

Most important, be positive. Don't unduly criticize anyone, especially your own child. If you criticize another player, chances are his parents are nearby. What purpose does this type of outburst serve? Don't take out your frustrations on a kid when he makes a mistake. It embarrasses both of you, and it only teaches the child to play less confidently. I guarantee that all kids will make mistakes and they will not improve if you punctuate the game with "What's the matter with you?" or "That was stupid!" or "If you don't get going, I'll. . . ." That kind of talk is disastrous.

If you cannot control yourself, then stay home. This may sound tough, but you will do a lot of damage to your child and to your relationship with your child if you don't control your anger. Some people just can't keep it in, so avoid damage by staying home. I've seen this problem often, and it really can screw a kid up. If you must yell, then say things like "Tough D," "Stay Low," or "Let's Go." Congratulate a good effort. Let the coach call the plays.

HOW TO TREAT THE COACH

First of all, the coach is giving up a lot of time to coach the team and deserves a lot of room. If you want to coach, sign up to do so or to help. Show up at practices or at club meetings to offer help. That earns you the right to give your opinion. Otherwise, be very conservative about offering it.

Second, realize your bias. You are a parent and you love your son. You may think that he deserves to play more or to play another position, but the coach knows a lot more about what all the kids can do and who has earned playing time. It's unfair for you to ask for more and unfair to the other kids for you to suggest that one of them should play less. Just work more with your child so he improves, and he will play more. Coaches want to win, and they usually give the better players more playing time.

However, coaches need to learn too. And sometimes they are going about things quite wrong. If this is the case, then gently indicate how you feel. It is important that you think about it a lot and make sure you know what you are talking about before you say anything. Question your own bias. If you still feel you can help, offer your opinion. Avoid an argument, or even a long debate. Make your point and ask the coach to think about it. Indicate that you are only trying to help. I strongly suggest not being argumentative. Say your piece, listen to the coach, then thank him for his time and end it. If you are lucky, the coach will be thankful. However, he may resent your interference and possibly even take it out on your child. If the situation becomes very bad, let your club president or school athletic director know how you feel. Keep in mind that if your child gets in the middle, he may suffer for it. If the experience is more damaging than good, remove your child from the team.

But remember, think about it, get advice, talk to other parents, and avoid being unduly disruptive. The point of football is to have fun—both watching and playing.

Chapter Ten

COACHING CHECKLIST

Take this book, or at least photocopy these pages. If you are a parent, watch your son when you go to a practice or a game. Look over the checkpoints one at a time and evaluate his performance. If you are a coach, bring it along to practice and look it over from time to time. It will help you focus your attention on possible problem areas.

DESIRE
☐ Drive for the ball.
☐ Hustle; play until the whistle.
☐ Never quit.

BLOCKING
Stance
☐ Drop sharply from ready to set positions.
☐ Set position—shoulder low and coiled.
☐ Legs shoulder-width or more apart.
☐ Weight moderately forward on hand.
☐ Down hand is inside back foot and just forward of shoulder, resting on the three interior fingers' knuckles, thumb back.
☐ Legs should be bent so the back is parallel to the ground.
☐ The tail should not be higher than the shoulders.
☐ The head should be up.
☐ The back should be straight, not curved.
☐ Bull the neck, eyes forward. Don't give away any clues.

Charge
☐ Explode instantly with the snap.
☐ Drive forward with the back foot.
☐ Stay low, legs wide, knees bent.
☐ Raise forearms toward opponent's chest, elbows out.

☐ Angle, don't step, to opposite side.

☐ Adjust for stunts.

Jolt

☐ Slam shoulder into opponent *hard*.

☐ Drive, don't lunge.

☐ Straighten legs on contact.

☐ Keep eyes open wide, head up.

☐ Sustain the block.

☐ Keep legs wide.

☐ Bring back leg up under the body.

☐ Move into the opponent's pressure.

☐ Drive forward with short, choppy steps.

☐ Turn opponent away and then back to scrimmage.

Specialty blocks

☐ Trap.

☐ Cross-body block.

☐ Crab block.

☐ Double-team.

☐ Pass block.

TACKLING

Stance

☐ Similar to blocker, but more weight forward.

☐ Low under the opponent.

☐ Inside foot back.

☐ Search for clues.

☐ Crouch on standing stance.

Tackling Techniques

☐ Explode off the snap.

☐ Neutralize the blocker's charge with the shoulder (to penetrate) or shiver. Give a jolt of your own.

☐ Shiver. Both palms thrust up into opponent's shoulder pads to keep opponent at bay.

☐ Stay under control.

☐ Drop to all fours if not blocked. Stack things up.
☐ Shed blocker at moment ballcarrier commits to one side.

Focus and wrap
☐ Drop or dip low.
☐ Focus on the belt.
☐ Legs wide and balanced.
☐ Drive shoulder into midsection. Jolt.
☐ Wrap arms tightly around the runner; try to smack the ball.
☐ Bring legs up quickly.
☐ Lift and then bring him down.
☐ If off-balance, tackle him any way possible.

PASSING

Quarterback Basics
☐ A foundation of good form is essential under pressure.
☐ Size up the defense. Where are the seams?
☐ Secure the snap with passing hand on top, fingers spread.
☐ Retreat quickly. Practice the footwork.
☐ Hold the ball high.
☐ Step forward into pocket.

Grip
☐ Snug but not a squeeze.
☐ Fingers spread wide, touching ball along the entire length.
☐ Hand back of center. Pinky is midball.
☐ Laces under last joint of fingers.
☐ Some space between palm and ball.
☐ Protect ball with free hand.

Release
☐ Stand erect, survey the field.
☐ Hold the ball high.
☐ Hit player as he breaks and is in a seam between defenders.
☐ Don't take too big a step. Step toward target.
☐ Snap the wrist; ball rolls off fingertips.
☐ Long pass. Tilt the nose up. Err long.

- ☐ Short pass. Nose even or down a bit; snap and throw hard. Err low and short.
- ☐ Jump pass. Adjust lead, release at top of jump. Try to get some forward momentum.

RECEIVING

Fundamentals

- ☐ Don't let the opponent delay you at the line.
- ☐ Run directly at the defender.
- ☐ Cut into pattern when he changes momentum to backpedal.
- ☐ Make a two- or three-step fake and quickly change direction.
- ☐ Stay under control. Save a bit of speed.
- ☐ React to the ball.
- ☐ Don't ignore the passer. Look to him.
- ☐ Focus on the ball.
- ☐ Don't reach too soon.
- ☐ Soft hands, fingers curled and spread.
- ☐ Catch it high, at front point or tip of the ball.
- ☐ Watch the ball all the way into the hands.
- ☐ Try to catch the ball while body is in the air.
- ☐ Recover and tackle if intercepted.
- ☐ Tuck the ball in before running.
- ☐ Change direction immediately.

RUNNING

Stance

- ☐ Feet spread wide outside shoulders.
- ☐ Very little weight on down hand.
- ☐ Focus straight ahead. Don't tip off the defense.

Pivot and snap

- ☐ Pivot first before stepping.
- ☐ Snap head and shoulders.
- ☐ Push off balls of the feet.
- ☐ First step is large one with foot on same side as play action.
- ☐ Look at the hole to see what is developing and let the quarterback worry about getting you the ball.

- [ ] Outside arm down across stomach, palm up, and the other arm elbow up across the chest on dive plays.
- [ ] Curl both hands around the tips of the ball.
- [ ] Carry the ball securely. Jam it into the pocket between the upper arm and ribs, forearm to the underside, fingers spread around the front top.
- [ ] Carry the ball in the arm farthest from the tackler, usually the arm closest to the nearest sideline.
- [ ] Run with power; run hard.
- [ ] Running maneuvers.
- [ ] Stiff arm. Just as tackler launches, place palm on shoulder or on top of helmet, lock arm, hop on contact.
- [ ] Step out. Jab and then step or leap sharply away.
- [ ] Pivot or spin. Give a leg and take it away with 360-degree spin, then change direction.
- [ ] Cross over. Lean and lift leg away from tackler.

SPECIALTIES

Snap to quarterback
- [ ] Feet wide, hips high, legs even.
- [ ] Weight moderately on the ball.
- [ ] Head and arm may be in neutral zone.
- [ ] Tilt ball as needed.
- [ ] Timing is critical.
- [ ] Quick firm snap to the hands, laces to fingertips.
- [ ] Step forward with the snap.
- [ ] Angle head and jolt.

Snap for punts and placekicks
- [ ] Hold ball up front with a passer's grip.
- [ ] Raise the front point of the ball.
- [ ] Weight forward moderately on the ball.
- [ ] Guide it with the left hand; this hand leaves the ball first.
- [ ] Brace and step forward with the snap.
- [ ] Drive ball back with quick snapping action.
- [ ] Aim for belt of the punter or hands of the placekick holder.
- [ ] Snap with speed. Time is precious—take as little as possible.

☐ Focus on the snap, not the opponent.

Punting

☐ Look only at the ball as it is snapped.

☐ Feet parallel, weight on left foot.

☐ Arms extended outward, palms down and inward, thumbs up, fingers spread.

☐ Stand erect, hands soft, body relaxed.

☐ Let the snap come all the way to the hands.

☐ Withdraw and soften hands to receive the ball.

☐ Place the laces up; right hand back cradling the ball.

☐ Serve, don't drop ball to foot. Use right hand.

☐ Tip of ball points down and inside a bit.

☐ Spiral comes if kicked with right side of the foot, to the right of shoelaces, a hair off-center. Contact belly of ball.

☐ End-over-end kick if ball is kicked directly on the instep.

☐ Snap the locked ankle forward to give power and distance.

☐ Point the toe forward.

☐ Concentrate on point of contact.

☐ Follow through enough to pull the body forward a hop.

Placekicking

☐ Take two or three steps, depending on distance.

☐ Kick soccer style.

☐ Stand with legs nearly even, leaning forward on front foot while waiting for snap.

☐ Approach ball in a quarter-circle motion.

☐ Plant toes of free foot even with back of ball, a few inches to the side, pointing at the target.

☐ Concentrate on point of contact.

Receiving punts and kickoffs

☐ Judge where the ball will land.

☐ Catch it moving forward.

☐ Arms raised outward, upward a bit, palms up, fingers spread, hands fairly close together.

☐ Catch with hands and bring quickly into body.

☐ Soften hands and body for the catch.

APPENDIX: SUMMARY OF PENALTIES

LOSS OF 5 YARDS
1. Failure to properly wear required equipment during a down.
2. Delay of game.
3. Failure to properly wear required equipment prior to snap.
4. Illegal substitution.
5. Encroachment.
6. Free kick infraction.
7. Invalid or illegal fair catch signal.
8. False start or any illegal act by snapper.
9. Fewer than seven on offensive line or a numbering violation.
10. Illegal formation or procedure at snap.
11. Illegal motion or shift.
12. Illegal handing ball forward (also loss of down).
13. Illegal forward pass (if by offense, loss of down also).
14. Intentional grounding (also loss of down).
15. Ineligible receiver downfield.
16. Helping runner.
17. Attendant illegally on field.
18. Nonplayer outside of the team box but not on field.

LOSS OF 10 YARDS
1. Illegal blocking technique.
2. Illegal use of hands.
3. Interlocked blocking.
4. Holding.
5. Runner grasping a teammate.
6. Striking blocker's head with hand(s).

LOSS OF 15 YARDS
1. Fair catch interference.
2. Illegal block after valid or invalid fair catch signal.
3. Forward pass interference (also loss of down if by offense; a first down if by defense). If intentional or unsportsmanlike, an additional 15 yards.
4. Illegal block below the waist or on free kicker or holder.
5. Clipping.
6. Chop block.
7. Tripping.
8. Charging into an opponent obviously out of the play.
9. Piling, hurdling, unnecessary roughness, personal fouls.
10. Grasping opponent's face protector or any helmet opening.
11. Butt block, face tackle or spear.
12. Roughing the passer (also a first down).
13. Roughing the kicker or holder (also a first down).
14. Unsportsmanlike conduct by player or nonplayer.
15. Illegal participation.
16. Illegal kicking or batting the ball.
17. Nonplayer illegally on field.

Striking, kicking, kneeing, or any act, if unduly rough or flagrant, may result in disqualification.

GLOSSARY—TALKING FOOTBALL

Adornments: Uniform adornments that serve no purpose or are distracting are illegal. You see adornments from time to time in the Pros but not often at the youth level.

Backfield: The quarterback and running backs constitute the offensive backfield. There are tailbacks (deep in the backfield), flanker backs (spread outside of the end), wingbacks (spread out behind the end), single or lone backs (when there is only one running back behind the quarterback), and others based on regional terminology. The defensive backfield is called the *secondary*.

Ball: A high school football must be four-paneled, pebble-grain, tan cowhide with eight or twelve evenly spaced laces. It should be 10⅞ to 11⁷⁄₁₆ inches long with a 20¾ to 21¼ inch middle circumference and a 27¾ to 28½ inch long circumference. It must weigh 14 to 15 ounces and be inflated to 12½ to 13½ pounds per square inch. At youth levels the ball can be a bit smaller in most dimensions. Thus the length can be 10 to 11 inches, the middle circumference can be 19 to 20 inches, the long circumference can be 26 to 27 inches, the weight can be 12 to 14 ounces, and inflation can be 12½ to 13½ pounds per square inch.

Bat: In a few instances batting a ball by hand is legal. A player can bat a pass, kick or fumble in flight if he is attempting to block. He can also bat a kicked ball forward before he or the ball goes into the opponent's end zone to avoid a touchback.

Belly: A deception move in which the quarterback holds the ball in the belly of a running back before withdrawing or releasing it. Thus the quarterback momentarily "rides the belly" while deciding what to do based on what the defense does.

Blitz: A defensive move by a member of the secondary (linebacker, cornerback or safety) in which the player leaves his zone and rushes through a gap to the quarterback, hoping to tackle him or the ballcarrier so there is a loss of yardage. The move has some danger in that the blitzer's defensive zone is left exposed.

Blocking: The act of impeding a defensive player by moving him from the path of the ballcarrier or interfering with his ability to make a tackle. Types of blocks include: *cross-blocks*, when two offensive linemen cross in front of each other and block each other's man; *cross-body blocks*, in which a blocker hurls his body horizontally across the chest of a defender; *shoulder blocks*, or jolts; *open field blocks*, in which one blocks a defender downfield; and *screens,* in which a blocker simply gets between a defender and the ballcarrier. A running back who blocks well is often called a blocking back. Defenders also try to *block* or bat punts and place-kicks.

Bootleg: A deception move in which the quarterback fakes a handoff to a running back and then, hiding the ball by his hip, runs wide around the end to gain yardage. Often the quarterback runs casually at first, pretending he doesn't have the ball to perpetuate the fake, and then he suddenly speeds up.

Buck: Running hard into the middle of the line, often on a short yardage situation.

Buttonhook: The receiver runs straight ahead for 5 to 7 yards, then wheels and turns to face the quarterback for a pass. The buttonhook is often a timing pass and the ball meets the receiver as soon as he stops and turns. A great fake move, if the quarterback has time, is for the receiver to break downfield just after the defender approaches. It's a bread-and-butter touchdown play.

Center: The offensive lineman who snaps (or centers) the ball to the quarterback. He is usually found in the center of the offensive line and generally has a number in the 50s.

Chain gang: A group of three field assistants, one of whom is responsible for holding the down marker, a tall pole with cards displayed on the top to signify which down it is. This person places the pole on the new line of scrimmage on each play. The other two handle the chains, which are two tall poles separated by a ten-foot chain. The distance between these poles is the distance that must be covered to get a first down. At youth levels, chain gang members are parents who are pressed into service along the sideline.

Cheerleaders: Those young people who stir up both fans and players. They add much to the spirit of competition and to what football is all about.

Clipping: Blocking an opponent from behind and below the waist outside a free blocking zone (see below). Clipping carries a fifteen-yard penalty. If the block is above the waist, the penalty is 5 yards and the block is called *illegal use of the hands.*

Counter: A play design in which the offensive backs flow in one direction, then one cuts back to run the ball in the other direction.

Cutback: A runner's move when he crosses the line of scrimmage in a certain direction and then cuts back in the other direction as he penetrates the defense. A cutback is like a counter except that it occurs spontaneously and after the runner crosses the line of scrimmage.

Dead ball spot: The spot under the foremost point of the ball when it becomes dead by rule—that is, when the runner steps on or over the sideline or when his knee touches the ground. In the Pros, the ball is dead when the runner's knee touches the ground as a result of contact with an opponent. If a runner slips in the Pros, he can get up again and run if he was not touched. The place where the official spots the ball is often a source of sideline grumbling, since it often determines whether a team keeps the ball or loses possession.

Defense: The attempt to stop the other team from advancing the ball.

Dive: A running play up the middle in the gap between the center and the guard. It is a quickly moving play that is usually run by a strong back, the fullback.

Double-team: Assigning two blockers to one defender in a coordinated block, usually done when a defender is very strong and is giving the offense too much trouble.

Down: A down is a play. A team gets four downs to move the ball 10 yards. If they succeed, they get four more downs. If they fail, the other team gets the ball.

Draw: A play that tries to draw the defense into the backfield by delaying the handoff to the running back. Then, as a defender charges, he is hit in the side by a predesigned trap block and the runner is then free to advance. The delay gives the blocker time to pull and get to the defender.

Dropkick: Dropping the ball on its tip point and kicking it immediately as it begins to bounce up. Dropkicks are not used much anymore; they are tricky to do, so most teams sacrifice a potential blocker to hold the ball. Placekicks are now universally considered to be the best way to kick field goals and points-after-touchdown.

Dummy: Players who hold dummy or blocking pads in practice to allow blockers to run through their plays and work on blocking.

Encroachment: Having any part of the body inside the neutral zone at the snap of the ball.

End: The offensive or defensive player who positions himself at either end of the front line. On offense, an end in close to the rest of the line is called a tight end; otherwise he's a split end. Ends usually have numbers in the 80s.

End zone: The area covering 10 yards past the goal line. A pass caught in the end zone is a touchdown. The goalposts are located at the back of the end zone.

Equipment: Pop Warner and National Federation rules require a helmet certified by the National Operating Committee on Standards for Athletic Equipment (NOCSAE) with a visible warning label, a properly fastened chin strap, a multiple-bar face protector of nonbreakable material, shoulder pads, hip pads with tailbone protector, thigh guards, kneepads, mouth guard with a keeper strap, and an athletic supporter. I recommend that players wear a cup, sanctioned forearm pads and shin guards, and neck braces, even though they are not currently required. Kids may not wear any hard substance such as a cast or knee brace unless the hard surface is covered by ½-inch thick, closed cell, slow recovery rubber.

Extra point: At youth levels, the point after touchdown may be attempted from the 3 yard line. If the ball is placekicked through the goalposts, two points are scored in Pop Warner play.

Fair catch: By raising his hand above his head quickly and clearly, a player may receive a punt or placekick without being tackled. He may not, however, advance the ball, and a muffed catch results in a live ball.

Field goal: When a team has a fourth down and is close to the goal line, they can opt to placekick the ball through the uprights for three points. It doesn't happen often at the youth level because the kids don't placekick with accuracy yet.

First down: The first in each series of four chances to move the ball 10 yards.

Flag: A yellow penalty cloth that an official keeps in his back pocket and throws in the air to designate a rule violation.

Flea-flicker: A play in which the quarterback hands off to a running back who then flicks the ball *back* to the quarterback for a pass play. The objective is to fool the defense into thinking it is a running play so they leave pass receivers unguarded.

Forward pass: The ball may be thrown forward from behind the line of scrimmage to an eligible receiver (an end or a back). Once past the line of scrimmage, the ball may only be thrown laterally or backward.

Forward progress: This represents the point at which the ball is placed after a play, marking the forward-most point of a runner's progress before he was involuntarily knocked backward. If a receiver backs up voluntarily he loses any forward progress that he had gained beyond the point of the tackle.

Free blocking zone: A rectangular area extending 4 yards laterally and 3 yards forward and behind each scrimmage line from the point of the ball. In this zone an offensive player who was stationary at the snap and all defensive players may contact an opponent below the waist or from the rear.

Fullback: A running back. Usually he is the strongest running back, used for short-yardage dives up the middle. Fullbacks usually have numbers in the 30s.

Fumble: Dropping the football before the play ends, usually due to a hard tackle. Cannot be caused by contact with the ground. A fumble is a live ball; whoever recovers it gains possession.

Gaps: The spaces between offensive linemen through which the ball is carried. Defensive players must think of filling the gaps.

Goal line: The thick white lines marking the ends of the 100-yard playing surface. If any point of the ball breaks the vertical plane of this line, a touchdown is scored.

Goalposts: One of the two uprights of the goal that is situated in the center of each end line. The goalposts are connected by a crossbar that is 10 feet above the ground and 23 feet, 4 inches long. The uprights may be 4 inches thick and extend no less than 10 feet above the crossbar. The lower goalposts, if the goal is H-shaped, or post, if the goal is y-shaped (slingshot), must be padded. A wind directional streamer may be atop one of the uprights.

Guard: An interior lineman on offense who lines up next to the center. The middle person on the defensive line is called a noseguard. Guards usually wear numbers in the 60s.

Halfbacks: The faster running backs, usually lined up behind and to one side of the quarterback for wide running plays. Halfbacks usually wear numbers in the 40s.

Halftime: After two ten-minute quarters (at the Pop Warner level) there is a fifteen-minute halftime break. The Pros recently reduced this break to twelve minutes to speed up the game.

Hash marks: Also called the inbound line, these markings are 24 inches in length and form two broken lines down the field, 53 feet, 4 inches from each sideline, dividing the field longitudinally into thirds. When a ball goes out of bounds or is downed near a sideline, it is centered on the nearest hash mark. This gives the team some running room to each side on every play.

Huddle: Players gather before each play in a circle or other formation to receive the play instructions from the quarterback.

Incompletion: A forward pass that is not caught or not possessed by the receiver for a full step.

Ineligible receiver: Only the ends or backs may be downfield to receive a pass. This violation often occurs on punts when an interior lineman breaks downfield before the ball is punted.

Interception: A pass reception by the defense. It's the dream and the glory of the defensive back.

Interference: Called against the offense or defense for interfering with a player who is trying to receive a pass, usually by bumping or grabbing his hands before the ball gets to him. Incidental contact between two players who are both looking at and trying to catch a pass is not interference. The judgment is always whether the player was playing the receiver or the ball.

Kickoff: The free kick that starts the game and the second half. It also occurs after each touchdown or successful field goal and is kicked from the kicking team's 40 yard line. A kickoff return is the formation used by the receiving team to return the ball.

Lateral: A sideways or backward pass. It can be thrown at any time from any place on the field and usually is used to avoid a tackle.

Linebackers: The defensive personnel immediately behind defensive linemen. Linebackers are usually both agile and strong, and they are great tacklers. They often wear numbers in the 50s or 90s.

Man-to-man: A pass defense term that designates individual coverage. Each defensive back is assigned to stay with a specific offensive receiver on a pass play.

Midfield: The 50 yard line, marked by a stripe across the center of the field. Seats on the 50 yard line are considered to be the best in the house.

Muff: An unsuccessful attempt to recover a fumble.

Neutral zone: An imaginary belt across the field formed by the nose tip and back point of the football as it rests with its foremost tip on the line of scrimmage.

Offense: The team with possession of the ball; they attempt to advance the ball and score.

Officials: There are usually four officials in a high school crew. I've seen Pop Warner games with only two or three. The *referee* is in charge— he keeps score, supervises the conduct of the game, and keeps the game

OFFICIAL SIGNALS

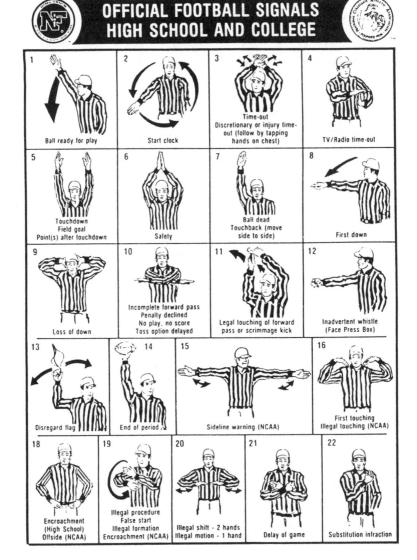

OFFICIAL FOOTBALL SIGNALS
HIGH SCHOOL AND COLLEGE

1. Ball ready for play
2. Start clock
3. Time-out Discretionary or injury time-out (follow by tapping hands on chest)
4. TV/Radio time-out
5. Touchdown Field goal Point(s) after touchdown
6. Safety
7. Ball dead Touchback (move side to side)
8. First down
9. Loss of down
10. Incomplete forward pass Penalty declined No play, no score Toss option delayed
11. Legal touching of forward pass or scrimmage kick
12. Inadvertent whistle (Face Press Box)
13. Disregard flag
14. End of period
15. Sideline warning (NCAA)
16. First touching Illegal touching (NCAA)
18. Encroachment (High School) Offside (NCAA)
19. Illegal procedure False start Illegal formation Encroachment (NCAA)
20. Illegal shift - 2 hands Illegal motion - 1 hand
21. Delay of game
22. Substitution infraction

OFFICIAL SIGNALS

clock. He decides differences of opinion. He usually lines up on the offensive side of scrimmage and primarily decides forward progress of the ball. The *umpire* is responsible for penalty administration and lines up on the defensive side of scrimmage. The *linesman* covers action in the neutral zone and stands on the line of scrimmage. He looks for pass interference in his side of the field. The *line judge* is on the opposite side from the linesman. The official signals are found in Figures 50A & 50B.

Offside: Crossing the line of scrimmage before the ball is snapped. The penalty for this violation is a loss of 5 yards.

Off-tackle: The gap between the tackle and the end and a popular place for running plays.

Option: A popular play at youth and high school levels, even in some colleges. A quarterback sweeps around an end with another running back just off his outside shoulder. He can keep the ball or lateral it to the other back depending on how the defense reacts. An option pass play is a sweep by a halfback who has the option of passing the ball or continuing the run, again depending on how the defense reacts. Triple option plays include an optional belly dive before the option sweep.

Penalties: A penalty is the consequence of an infraction of the rules of football. It is measured in increments of 5, 10 or 15 yards against the team that committed the foul. It may be awarded from the place of infraction, the line of scrimmage, or the end of a run, depending on the infraction. It may also be declined by the other team. See Appendix for a summary of penalties.

Pile-up: Piling on a tackled ballplayer is illegal. However, the forward momentum of tacklers often carries several to a pileup.

Pitchout: A play designed to get a halfback to the outside very quickly. On a sweep play the ball is pitched to him as he darts to the outside.

Placekick: Kicking a ball in a kickoff, a field goal, or a point after touchdown when the ball is held in place for a teammate.

Platoon: Having different players on the offensive team than those on the defense. At youth levels the best players play both ways.

Pocket: An area formed by the offensive pass blockers in front and to the side of the quarterback in a pass play.

Point after touchdown (PAT): A team may score one or two additional points after a touchdown. At youth levels two are scored on a placekick between the uprights, and one is scored on a rush or pass into the end zone. The line of scrimmage for PAT is the 3 yard line.

Post pass: A deep pass across the middle, toward the goalpost. Also called a *Hail Mary* or a *bomb.*

Punt: A ball kicked to the opponent by dropping it onto the foot. This usually is the method for exchanging possession on fourth down.

Pursuit: The defensive act of pursuing the ballcarrier on an intercept angle, even if the play goes away from the defender.

Quarter: The game is divided into four time periods called quarters, usually ten minutes each at pre-high-school levels. There is a one- to two-minute period between quarters and a fifteen-minute halftime. High school games are for four twelve-minute quarters.

Quarterback: The offensive captain and field general who calls the plays. He takes the snap and either hands off the ball to a running back or passes it. The quarterback usually wears a number from 1 to 19.

Razzle-dazzle: Intricate or funny play patterns such as end around, reverse, flea-flicker or option. These involve tricky handoffs and often take a lot of precision but can break for big plays.

Replay: A videotaped copy of a football play. Replays are used in the Pros to review an official's call. They are not used at any other level and are a matter of some controversy.

Reverse: A razzle-dazzle play in which a running back runs to one side, pulling the defense with him, and then hands off the ball to another player going the other way.

Roll-out: Instead of staying in the pass protection "pocket," an agile quarterback can run off to one side to gain time for his receivers to get free for a pass. This is a *scramble* if not designed ahead of time.

Sack: Tackling a quarterback behind the line of scrimmage. This is the dream of every pass rusher.

Safety: (a) The deepest defensive back. (b) A tackle in a team's own end zone resulting in two points and a free kick to the opponent.

Scramble: The move a quarterback often makes to avoid onrushing tacklers when his protection breaks down.

Screen pass: A play that allows the defensive line to rush the quarterback freely, as a ploy. The quarterback then lofts a short pass over the charging defenders to a receiver who lines up just behind the waiting offensive linemen.

Scrimmage: (a) The imaginary line across the field that runs through the point of the front tip of the ball. (b) A practice football game.

Secondary: The defensive backfield.

Shift: Offensive backs and defenders are allowed to shift position and change alignment, individually or as a unit, before the ball is snapped. Offensive players must be set for one second before the snap (one player may legally be in motion).

Shiver: A useful defensive weapon, thrusting the hands forward, palms forward, into a blocker's shoulders to keep him at bay and thus not allowing him access to the defender's body.

Shoestring tackle: It is preferable to tackle hard with the shoulder, but when the ballcarrier is breaking away the defensive player should grab for the feet.

Shotgun: An offensive formation in which the quarterback lines up 4 to 5 yards behind the center to receive the snap. This is used on obvious passing situations and helps the quarterback gain a few seconds. Since he need not drop back, he can more readily focus on the secondary and the pass pattern.

Sidelines: The white stripes lengthwise down the sides of the field. These lines are out-of-bounds to any body part.

Signals: The hiking cadence and instructions called by a quarterback at the line of scrimmage. A typical one is "Down—Green—242—Set—Hike 1—Hike 2—Hike 3." "Down" signifies that the team should get in the ready position. "Green" is a code that signals if the play will be changed and is followed by the new play. The "set" signal gets the linemen into set position. The ball is hiked on a number called in the huddle.

Slant: A block to one side, or a running play off-tackle or off-guard.

Snap: The backward hike of the ball from the center between his legs to the quarterback or other person (punter, placekick holder).

Spin: A move by a running back as he is about to be tackled. With a good spin a back can break free from a mediocre tackle.

Stance: The position of a player when the ball is the snapped. Stances are designed to ready each person for his particular job and vary according to that task.

Straight-arm: A useful weapon for a running back is to stiff-arm, palms outward, onto the shoulder of a would-be tackler. A "hop" upon contact can often launch a runner, using the tackler's momentum, for several feet.

Stunts: Defensive moves to confuse blocking assignments by having linemen switch charging lanes when the ball is snapped.

Submarine: A low, diving defensive line move to get under a block and into a gap. The player then pulls his legs up quickly to meet the ballcarrier.

Substitution: The substitution rules are fairly unrestricted. Any number of players may enter or leave between downs. No more than eleven players may be on the field at one time, although it is not illegal to have fewer. Eleven players are needed to start, but not finish, a game in high school.

Sweep: A running play that heads wide laterally and endeavors to run around the defense.

Tackle: A lineman on offense or defense who plays inside the end. Linemen are usually the biggest players on the team and their numbers are in the 70s. This term also designates the art of bringing a ballcarrier to his knees.

Tailback: The deepest running back.

Timeout: Either side may stop the clock after any play three times per half. This is usually done by the team in possession of the ball to delay the half from ending so they have a chance to score. It's also used to talk things over before an important play. In youth levels it's used a lot to stop the twenty-five-second clock from expiring while waiting for a player to get back on the field.

Timing pass: A prearranged pass pattern in which the quarterback throws to an area before the receiver actually turns (or stops). It is usually too sophisticated for most youth teams.

Touchback: A punt or kickoff that goes into the end zone and is downed there by the team who will take possession. A touchback also occurs when a fumbled ball is recovered or a pass is intercepted in the offensive end zone by the defense and no attempt is made to run it out. They then get the ball on the 20 yard line.

Touchdown: Breaking the plane of the goal line with the ball. This can be achieved by running the ball over the goal line or catching a pass in the end zone. It is the primary objective of football and scores six points.

Trapping: Blocking a player from the side after allowing him to advance beyond the line of scrimmage.

Unbalanced line: An offensive line with more linemen on one side of the center than on the other.

Water boy: An important sideline job to avoid dehydration.

Wingback: A running back who lines up outside the offensive end.

Zone defense: When the pass defense protects a certain territory rather than defending man-to-man.

INDEX